God of War Complete Guide & Walkthrough

D1531150

Mrs. Eulah Manh

ISBN: 979-8-4020-7364-7

CONTENTS

Our guide for God of War contains all necessary information that will help you complete the game in 100%. Content-wise, this is a large game. It is full of secrets, optional challenges and collectibles - this guide will help you complete all of them. You will find Nornirn chests, Odin's Ravens, Lore Markers or Artefacts. We have created a richly illustrated walkthrough that will help you complete all main missions. You can also find out how to reach secret realms, defeat 9 hidden bosses (valkyrie) and learn the gameplay basics. The God of War returns on PC 2022!

TIPS AND TRICKS

Tips for Starting Out

God of War can be a bit challenging, but there are a few things you can do to make the grand Nordic adventure easier on yourself.

Break Everything

Those pots, boxes, and random holders lying around may seem harmless, however in some cases you'll track down Healthstones, and surprisingly more critically, Hacksilver! The greater part of these finds are measly, yet additional time your endeavors will add up to an incredible fortune. Now and then however, you'll be fortunate and track down a crowd of hundreds or even thousands concealed in odd spots.

Sell Stuff

Talking about tracking down Hacksilver, there's not a remotely good excuse to clutch the Artifacts you find. Sell them for heaps of money from the beginning. Look at our Walkthrough so you don't miss any as you play.

Get Those Collectibles

There are something beyond Artifacts to scour for in the Nine Realms. There are likewise Nornir Chests (the chests locked with runes), which award wellbeing bar and fury bar boosts;Legendary Chests, with Runic Attacks inside; Odin's Ravens, which award XP as a feature of a Labor, and a couple of more which make certain to assist you with becoming more grounded. Look out and investigate.

Focus on Labors

You can see a rundown of Labors under the Goals tab in the menu. They carry on like a bunch of difficulties that open as you go over new adversaries and an assortment of different things on the planet. Remember them as you proceed with your excursion so you can effectively pursue acquiring that sweet extra XP they award.

Use Your XP

It's worth focusing on that XP doesn't influence Kratos' or alternately Atreus' level. You need to utilize the XP you procure for it to matter! Sometimes, actually look at the Skills tab, and SPEND the XP. You can tab over the various segments with the D-Pad. XP might appear to be scant from the outset, however you'll be swimming in it ultimately, so use it on the Skills connected with the assaults you the most.

Some of the time, Be a Coward

Infrequently you'll run into an unwell foe that is a couple of levels above you. Assuming you're resolved to killing it, take a stab at staying away - I mean, truly, remain as distant as could be expected - and consistently toss your Leviathan Ax at the foe's weakpoints in the event that it has them. Likely not generally so invigorating as close-went battle, yet at the same certainly more secure and more dependable.

Meandering Doesn't Mean You're Lost

Assuming you're struggling, accept Atreus' recommendation and redirect outside of what might be expected of the Region you're in. There are a huge load of stowed away regions open by boat in the Lake of Nine, for instance.

Do some investigating, and you might leave with a few uncommon Armor, Enchantments, Runic Attacks, or Ax Pommels. Furthermore, a lot of extra XP for additional abilities and Hacksilver for better Armor!

Purchase and Upgrade Armor

Like XP, don't be parsimonious with Hacksilver. Since XP doesn't influence you're strength, all of your details are dependent on your stuff. You can determine whether another piece of Armor or Upgrade will emphatically or adversely sway Kratos' level by the green (positive) or red (negative) triangles that show up close to the level in the Shop menu.

Note that most reinforcement can be redesigned (for undeniably short of what it costs for the underlying buy), yet they will ultimately arrive at a cap. Therefore, you might need to zero in on purchasing or observing one to be set of covering to completely update dependent on your detail inclinations - then, at that point, trust that more protective layer will open up as the story advances to purchase and overhaul another set as better levels become accessible.

You can generally get more Hacksilver, so use it!

Try not to Neglect Atreus

We don't mean in a real sense, however focus on his gear and Skills as much as Kratos'. His shield gives him additional capacities that will help you in battle, such as passing you Healthstones or offering you chances to cause additional harm.

Buying his Skills makes Atreus significantly more valuable and dynamic in battle too. Besides, Atreus' stuff is by and large altogether less expensive to buy than Kratos', so get to it. You'll think twice about it assuming you pause, and with enough ability and stuff put resources into him, he'll become one of the most valuable instruments in your munititions stockpile.

Associate After Fighting

At the point when an adversary is near, things that are typically ready to be connected with will not seem, by all accounts, to be so. The circle symbol actually won't appear, and you will not have the option to squeeze circle to accomplish something regardless of whether you realize you can. Along these lines, after you've completed a battle, try to glance around again in the event that you passed something you can get.

Combat Tips

Learn enemy attack patterns to make fights easier. Some of the heavy hitters actually have fewer attacks if you stand closer to them. Experiment to see what works best for you.

New foes regularly produce mid-fight, so be aware of your environmental factors. A white bolt marker will show up on Kratos when another danger shows up on the combat zone. That sign becomes red when the foe is in assaulting range.

Joining barehanded assaults with Atreus' bolts can develop a foe's paralyze meter amazingly rapidly. Start squeezing square at the same time with your assault buttons when your objective is executing a foe. This is especially useful for fast foes like the Revenant or adversaries that recover wellbeing rapidly.

Kratos doesn't take harm while playing out a R3 takedown.

Use abilities like Countering Strike or runic assaults that opposition foes to excursion more modest adversaries off the sides of precipices. This is particularly useful toward the beginning of intense fights.

Figure out how to repel. Certain abilities will explicitly expand repel harm or assemble combos dependent on repelling. Assuming that you're down to one straightforward foe, you can utilize it to assist you with getting down repel timing.

You can't repel assaults that are featured in red.

A weighty hatchet toss can freeze foes on the off chance that it hits them perfectly located. Follow it up with a R2 kick into a divider for gigantic harm, or kick them into different adversaries to incur those in the space of impact with ice.

Focus on your foe's legs then, at that point, utilize a light or speedy hatchet toss to trip them. They'll remain down for a brief timeframe, permitting you to zero in on others or hammer that fallen foe with a progression of weighty assaults. This is especially helpful against adversaries with safeguards assuming you don't have the safeguard slam expertise.

Assuming Kratos is feeling the loss of his hatchet the Triangle button shows on the base left overlay.

Kratos can do an avoid evade in a center of a combo and afterward still proceed with a similar combo chain. This is known as an avoid offset, and doing as such permits you to finish a long combo, as R1, R1, R1, R2, without remaining fixed. So you can press R1, R1, avoid, R1, R2.

Continuously search for valuable chances to utilize the climate for your potential benefit. You can lead adversaries to edges, evade around them, and afterward shuffle them off. Or on the other hand crush foes into dividers for enormous shock harm.

Peruse your Labors to all the more likely figure out how to involve the climate for your potential benefit in a battle. For instance, there's a Labor that requires Kratos to stick adversaries to dividers.

A few foes have executions that give a gigantic assistance in battle. Bad dreams can be tossed at different foes for an unstable shot, Ogres can be ridden and coordinated to crash gatherings of more modest adversaries, weighty draugrs can be utilized as battering rams, and more modest draugrs/hel walkers make a ring of shoot/ice that hits close by foes when executed.

Remember to involve your Runic assaults and change them as you experience various types of foes. Runic assaults can incur natural status infirmities as well, which can help delayed down extreme foes.

In the event that you or Atreus thump down an adversary, utilize a weighty assault (hold down R2) to cause enormous harm to your enemy and get a cool movement.

Attempt to pick Runic assaults that chain together well. For example, assuming you have an assault that paralyzes a line of adversaries, follow it up with something that has a huge area of impact and causes a great deal of harm.

Large foes like savages can hurt more modest adversaries when they assault.

Green elixirs are decisively situated in pots close to significant experiences. Be aware of your wellbeing bar before you get them. Leaving them on the guide until you really want them is vital to beating bigger adversary experiences.

On default controls, click R3 in a fight to zero in on a solitary adversary. This keep that target locked and permits you to turn around them. It additionally assists you land bow shots from a distance with Atreus.

Rage Tips

Pop that Rage assuming it's full when you're falling short on wellbeing. You'll get some wellbeing back as you cause harm.

Rage assembles quick from the get-go since the meter is more limited, so use it as frequently as you really want it.

Increment your Rage meter by tracking down Horn of Blood Mead. You can find 9 in all of God of War, so make certain to open Nornir Chests as you track down them.

Drop Rage by squeezing L3+R3! It costs a tad of Rage to drop, however that's amount better compared to squandering it.

Large Rage drops you open further down the ability tree channel your Rage meter quicker.

Try not to utilize Rage when you're battling Revenant. Indeed, even in Rage, they move excessively fast for Kratos to land viable hits.

Wellbeing and Regen Tips

Assuming you're playing on a really difficult trouble level or then again on the off chance that you're struggling remaining alive in longer battles, make certain to purchase shield for Atreus that permits him to observe arbitrary wellbeing drops for Kratos.

Spiritualist Gates bring Kratos back up to full wellbeing!

Kratos recaptures wellbeing when he causes harm in Rage mode.

Harsh Squirrel is Atreus' mystery most supportive Runic Attack. You can observe it Tap to Reveal This capacity gathers an apparition squirrel named Ratatöskr (voiced by Troy Baker!) who will uncover Health and Rage consumables for you, causing him a deep sense of dismay. This allows you to re-energize your Rage and Health is very simple ways, yet it has a long cooldown.

Exploration Tips

Divine force of War's reality brings a lot to the table, including a few unquestionably supportive things concealed stealthily puts. Utilize these tips to ensure you're taking advantage of your excursion.

Truly, address the Nornir chest bewilders each time you experience them! This will help you to up your wellbeing and other significant assets from the

---

get-go in the game.

Utilize the Left-Hand rule! Assuming that you've at any point needed to settle a labyrinth without any pieces of information, you may have followed the "left-hand rule" (or "right-hand rule"). Fundamentally, embrace the dividers left - and consistently go left - assessing each inch en route. You'll discover anything you might have missed, so on the off chance that you're lost, give this a shot.

This might appear glaringly evident, however remember to gaze upward. You might observe something you can hit with Kratos' hatchet or shoot with Atreus' bolts to open a way or procure some extra Hacksilver.

When you're ready to investigate the Lake of the Nine, use your boat to investigate however much you can and be watching out for Yggdrasil's Dew. These award super durable rewards to your details and will give you an uncommon lift that isn't attached to equip.

Swing your hatchet into each pot and container you see. These might contain just a modest quantity of Hacksilver, yet everything develops over the long haul.

On the planned ringer based Nornir chest puzzles, consider tossing your hatchet behind the principal chime you wish to trigger, then, at that point, reviewing it when you are arranged for the second ringer in the succession. This can save you an important split second fundamental for finishing the test.

Domain Tears aren't all risky. Assuming you needed to do a riddle to uncover it or then again in the event that it's in a little region that wouldn't consider battling, it's most likely protected. It'll likewise appear on your guide as a Realm Tear rather than Realm Tear Encounter.

Assuming that you're hunting Odin's Ravens (Spies of Odin), tune in for a gleaming sound and cawing.

Gold and purple chests contain Ciphers expected to get to the domains of Muspelheim and Niflheim - 4 codes are needed to open a domain, however there are a very sizable amount of chests to find, as extra chests will give you Enchantments.

Skills and Leveling Tips

As mentioned, Kratos doesn't gain levels through XP – instead, you have to upgrade his armor. Below you'll find tips on how to upgrade Kratos' armor for levels and some tips on skills.

Skills

These are general tips, but if you're looking for which skills to upgrade first or essential skills, visit the Skills page for a complete guide.

If your skills glow in the skill tree then you've unlocked their bonus.

Atreus needs your consideration. It's to your greatest advantage to put resources into his development almost immediately!

Utilize the right weapon for the right experience - a few foes are invulnerable to the Leviathan Ax's frigid assaults, so use your clench hands all things being equal! Ensure you have the right abilities updated for that battle as well.

Never disregard redesigning Runic Attacks. Accumulating XP doesn't benefit you. Assuming you like an assault, redesign it to at minimum level 2 sooner than later.

Reinforcement and Weapons

You'll track down numerous Enchantments for your weapons assuming you investigate. Make a point to check their details and prepare the best ones continually to step up quicker.

Not all Armor is created - a few Armor Chests can be found in districts, concealed in Coffins that can be interesting to get to.

At times, completely redesigned lower level covering can be superior to un-updated shield of a higher level, so you might have to put resources into overhauling another set before it becomes helpful.

Overhaul your reinforcement with Enchantments when you can't bear to redesign your shield. It's likewise worth updating nice defensive layer for additional spaces. Regardless of whether your defensive layer is somewhat low, your charms can incredibly help your level in the event that they're sufficiently high and assuming you have a few prepared.

Deck out Atreus' protection to commend your playstyle. Give him the runic protection assuming you end up needing wellbeing continually, or the scuffle covering to benefit from him wrecking or gagging adversaries all the more regularly.

Like Runic assaults, change your Enchantments on the off chance that you're having inconvenience in specific battles.

Assuming you're struggling figuring out how to repel, prepare the Golden Talisman of Protection. The more you level it, the greater the repel window becomes. It must be evened out up to even out 5, however you should think that it is genuinely early.

Overhauling your Luck expands your opportunity to conceivably get a bigger number of dropped things from battles.

General Tips
In the event that you're not a devotee of the controls you can remap buttons in the menus.

There's a great deal of discourse in God of War, and some of it occurs in the hotness of fight. Turn on captions assuming you're struggling hearing Atreus' callouts or legend that is shared during battles.

If you're stuck fighting a new enemy or lost in a new area, Atreus will almost always hit at what you need to do next.

THINGS YOU SHOULD KNOW BEFORE PLAYING GOD OF WAR

Father has a Brand New Ax

Kratos likewise has another weapon this time around - the Leviathan Ax. It may not be very similar to the Blades of Chaos, however it tends to be utilized in an assortment of ways: performing light and weighty assaults and combos, freezing specific articles, and tossed at adversaries and the climate, which can be gotten back to you at the press of a button.

Indeed, even without his new hatchet, Kratos can likewise take part close by to-hand battle that might bargain less harm, yet can quickly paralyze foes to set up for a completing blow. He likewise has a retractable safeguard utilized for hindering approaching assaults, and can counterbalance adversaries by holding up the safeguard without a second to spare.

Battle is not generally zoomed out as it was in past titles, as now battle goes from over the shoulder in a lot more tight technique that will zoom out a piece as battle unfurls. Kratos can't lock on to adversaries, however can undoubtedly move between focuses with his assaults, and can do a speedy turn by holding down on the D-Pad. Indeed, even with a more engaged style, you can in any case string together combo assaults with weapons and Atreus' bolts, joined with shuffling adversaries in the air with weighty assaults or crushing them into the climate or one another.

The Realms of the North

While past titles in the God of War series were a touch more direct in plan, this God of War is somewhat more open - yet just partially.

The primary excursion that Kratos and his child set out on will take them through specific areas of Midgard. A considerable lot of these areas conceal collectibles, chests, and different things that can be found off in an unexpected direction or behind astounding contraptions - however the courses don't get too large.

Nonetheless, there are sure areas that open up to permit investigation over a more prominent region that conceals numerous different districts - and surprisingly covered up locales that can without much of a stretch be missed. These more modest regions aren't connected with your primary excursion, however frequently conceal collectibles, side journeys, and different secrets.

What's more, redesigns and capacities acquired after some time might open specific regions or fortunes that weren't accessible prior - like the Legend of Zelda or Tomb Raider.

The universe of the Norse public is still large enough that there are regions to cross by boat, and a kind of quick travel ultimately opens up.

Distraught Dad and his Rad Lad
Kratos' has a child named Atreus that will go along with him on his undertakings, and should rapidly figure out how to help his dad in battle.

While he gets going feeble, Atreus' battle capacities ought not be misjudged. With an order from Kratos, Atreus can shoot bolts that can harm and divert adversaries that Kratos is focusing on. Bolts terminated by order will drain his quiver, which re-energizes after some time.

As Atreus fills in capacity, he'll have the option to fast fire less harming bolts all alone, and divert, wreck, or stifle foes in close battle that can set up adversaries for Kratos to hit with a major assault.

Creating a Better God
As you experience through the domains of the Nordic Gods, you'll begin to observe money and making fixings that can be utilized at dwarven shops to make and overhaul an assortment of merchandise.

Here you can further develop your weapons for both Kratos and the kid, purchase covering, and update them to further develop their abilities. You'll likewise ultimately get attachments for protection that tradable charms can be put in.

This large number of things and more can be bought for the hacksilver you find in chests, urns, and on bodies, just as from overcoming adversaries. Certain shield and different things will likewise require explicit making parts to manufacture: Once you either track down these fixings or find the things that need them, you can check your assets page for more data on where to see as additional.

Acquiring Levels, and furthermore Experience

Kratos has a fascinating method of becoming more grounded throughout the span of your experience. There are two estimations: your level and your experience, that work in various ways.

Rather than acquiring experience to increment in level - experience is rather a kind of money used to buy abilities for your weapon capacities, and furthermore used to update specific Runic Abilities. Experience is acquired in numerous ways: from finishing missions and side journeys, tracking down collectibles, killing beasts, and that's only the tip of the iceberg.

Since experience doesn't factor into your general level, it is your weapons and shield that rather decide the level of Kratos' ability. As you find, prepare, and redesign your protection and weapon, you'll acquire focuses in the principle details that include:

Strength - expands harm for all assaults.

Runic - Increases both Runic Attack and Elemental harm.

Safeguard - Reduces all harm taken.

Imperativeness - Increases greatest wellbeing and diminishes time staggered from adversary assaults.

Karma - Increases perk initiation chance from Enchantments, and builds XP and hacksilver acquired.

Cooldown - Reduces re-energize season of Runic Attacks and Summons, just as Talismans.

your level and the details you have expanded will decide how powerful you are in battle against foes. In the event that you are close or over their level, their wellbeing bar will be green. Extreme foes have orange wellbeing bars, and those far over your power will have purple wellbeing bars.

There's no correct method for expanding your details, as various protective layer sets and charms offer distinctive detail rewards - it's dependent upon you to sort out which details you need to zero in on to mirror your playstyle.

God of War Complete Guide & Walkthrough

COMPLETE WALKTHROUGH

THE MARKED TREES

When you pick start your game and pick the trouble fit to your experience, you'll quickly assume responsibility for Kratos and press the brief to associate with a tree, prior to swinging your hatchet over and again to bring it down.

When the tree is felled, Kratos will get it, and you'll have the option to drop down the way to the waterway where Atreus pauses. Associate with the boat, and you'll before long be on your way down the stream. With the excursion set apart in your Goals diary, you can investigate get some knowledge into your goal.

Follow the River Downstream

It's a short boat excursion to get to your objective - simply steer along through the little passage until you arrive at the opposite side and communicate with the far moor to get back ashore and lift up the tree once more.

When you're back in charge of Kratos, simply follow Atreus as you follow the wrapping way up to their home, and Kratos will store the tree to start slashing it up, as Atreus heads inside.

After the story situation transpires, Kratos will allure his child to get his bow and bolts to chase deer. Atreus should be the principle tracker, so you'll be taking cues from him.

Chase with Atreus

Atreus will begin driving you down a way toward the North as he looks for deer. You can now control Kratos better, and investigate the yard around the home on the off chance that you need - in any case, you will not have the option to participate in battle at this time.

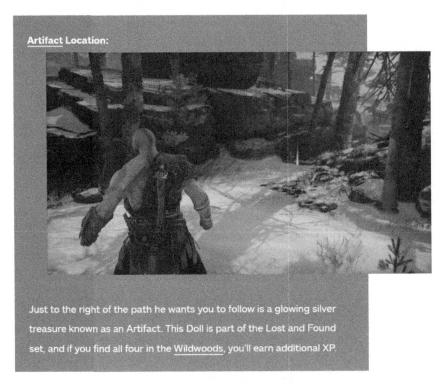

Artifact Location:

Just to the right of the path he wants you to follow is a glowing silver treasure known as an Artifact. This Doll is part of the Lost and Found set, and if you find all four in the Wildwoods, you'll earn additional XP.

Following Atreus up the way as he searches for tracks into a more extensive region. Atreus will move to the left - yet assuming you go right you can track down an alternate arrangement of tracks in the mud to bring up to the kid. As you move back to one side, Atreus will head up a few stone advances further into the wilds.

You can likewise check under the extension to track down a Hacksilver Chest - a ware you can use to overhaul things later.

Artifact Location:

Look to the left of the stone steps for another glowing icon that indicates another Artifact - the Boat is another part of the Lost and Found set.

Heading up from the steps you'll come to a hole you should leap to cross. After Atreus goes along with you, he'll recognize more tracks and take off running. In the end he'll track down the deer, and it will dash off additional North and to one side.

Prior to following the monster, make certain to look right where it originally seemed discover some Hacksilver on the ground, and a bigger Hacksilver Chest toward the finish of the way on the right.

As Atreus drives you to an extension, you can detect some Hacksilver by a precipice to one side - and a chain barely too far. Overlook it for the time being, and proceed across the scaffold until you observe the opposite end hindered.

Utilize the prompts to hold out your hatchet and focus on the barricade and toss it to break the wooden hindrance. In the wake of tossing it, you can return it to your hand whenever by squeezing triangle - recall this well.

On the opposite side of the scaffold, continue to climb until you spot the deer once more. After it runs off, Look right and you'll see Atreus get trapped by Draugr - presently it's at long last an ideal opportunity to battle.

With your Leviathan Ax, you can change among light and weighty assaults as you lock on to your objective - fights may appears to be increasingly slow calculated in contrast with Kratos' past undertakings, however you can in any case release a whirlwind of blows. An all around coordinated weighty assault can likewise send off an adversary in the air, permitting you to continue to hit with light assaults before they can hit the ground.

As more adversaries show up, you'll see that you have a retractable safeguard you can use to obstruct approaching assaults, and you can likewise toss your hatchet at foes, and proceed with the battle with safeguard and clench hand. Evaluate combos by cutting separated adversaries, tossing your hatchet at another objective, beating them, and sending your hatchet flying once more into your hand.

Whenever you've killed every one of the dangers, you can forge ahead to chase the deer. Prior to heading further, pivot back where Atreus attempted to shoot the deer to observe a low log you can jump over. You'll track down a body here with some Hacksilver you can get.

Entering the remnants, snatch the green Healthstone to recharge any wellbeing you lost. You can likewise admire spot a monster pail with a gleaming symbol above it that you can toss your hatchet at to send it crashing down for some Hacksilver. Atreus will follow the stag to the left, however you can go right to drop down to the option to track down a side way.

On the left of this way will be a Hacksilver Chest, and in the event that you continue to move to the stream, you can track down a body close to the cascade on the right with more Hacksilver, and a view beneath focuses to more fortunes to find.

Assuming you look to one side of the cascade you can detect that chain you saw before. Head back upstream to the principal cascade and search for an edge to move to the side prompting a pit fire with some Hacksilver.

Go right and you'll observe the foundation of the chain that you can descend to the stream. Down here, two Rabid Wolves will assault you - they move quick, be prepared to avoid or obstruct and afterward circle back to a couple of swipes, and don't get too anxious to even consider assaulting or allow one to get behind you.

Whenever you've managed them, look to one side to track down a gigantic Coffin that holds a great deal of Hacksilver.

Artifact Location:

After clearing out the wolves down in the ravine, look to the left to find the glowing icon where another Artifact lies.

It is a Horse, part of the Lost and Found collection in this area.

Idunn Apple Location:

Back at the ruins, head straight instead of left where the deer went to find a big chest called a **Nornir Chest**. The chest however is locked, and requires you to find and break the three rune seals that match the ones on the large tomb.

You can find the "C" looking rune to the right of the tomb, the "N" looking rune in a smaller coffin on the left.

If you turn around, look along the left wall to spot the "R" looking rune behind some rocks and bushes next to the stairs. Breaking them all will allow you to collect an Idunn Apple, which can increase your maximum health.

Returning the chase, follow Atreus as he tracks the stag across an extension towards a premonition sanctuary. Disregard the chests and plunder on the ice beneath, you'll get to them soon enough.

When you enter through the sanctuary doors, you'll again see the stag off somewhere out there, yet you'll have to draw nearer. Follow Atreus over a hole and down the steps to the lower region of the sanctuary.

Down in the open region, more Draugr will assault you close to the far entryway. Start the battle with an all around put hatchet toss and jump over to begin punching prior to yanking your hatchet back. Try out your evading and obstructing abilities - and recall that taking out your safeguard without a second to spare can paralyze a foe and leave them powerless against follow up.

When this gathering has been crushed, you'll need to track down a way through - above, about that treasure you saw before: pivot and head through the opened entryway at the far edge of the open space to take off onto the ice.

Over here you can detect the huge chest and other plunder, yet more Rabid Wolves watch it. Be prepared to avoid or impede when they plan to rush to get a benefit over them, and keep to speedy strikes so one of them doesn't intrude on you with their nibble assaults.

As they fall, more will show up, as will Draugr, continue to battle until no more appear, and you can take the Hacksilver on the ground, just as a Coffin brimming with Hacksilver.

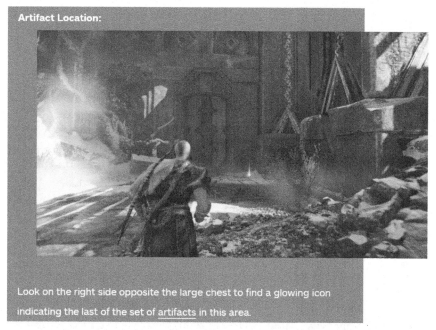

Artifact Location:

Look on the right side opposite the large chest to find a glowing icon indicating the last of the set of artifacts in this area.

The Viking Toy is the last of the Lost and Found set, which will net you a good reward of experience.

Back inside the sanctuary, search for a chain one of the two posts in the room.

Getting it will raise one of the two entryways before you, and the one to one side. Since giving up will bring down the entryway, you really want to make it stick. Gaze upward over the way to recognize a gleaming symbol (just as a can of Hacksilver) and hit them both to freeze the door (while as yet holding the chain) set up.

Presently you can go into the room on the option to open the Coffin loaded with Hacksilver, then, at that point, cross under the main raised entryway, and afterward return the Leviathan Ax to your side to bring down the door behind you and raise the external door.

Outside the sanctuary, Atreus will head right, yet you can go left to observe another enormous Coffin brimming with Hacksilver.

Pivot, and search for a recess close to the sanctuary door to observe a chain driving once more into the sanctuary.

Notice the red urn here close to some dark stone. Assuming you annihilate it (ideally a ways off) it will detonate with fire and explode the close by rock - and light you in fire on the off chance that you get excessively close.

Further up is an entryway impeded by rock, however you can detect a red urn on a chain on the opposite side. Remain back until you can see the opening to the opposite side, and thump down the pail of Hacksilver and afterward hit the chain's objective to send the urn crashing down, unblocking the door so you can arrive at a Hacksilver Chest.

Lore Location:

Head back and up the stairs from the chain that led you back into the temple, and you'll find a path leading up to a **Hacksilver Chest** on the right alcove, and a barricade dead ahead.

Past the barricade is a large ornate wooden **Jotnar Shrine**, which you can open to reveal the lore of Skoll and Hati, the wolf-giants that chase the sun and moon.

Get back to the sanctuary outside and follow the way upwards to a little bank neglecting the stag underneath.

Kratos will attempt to direct Atreus to strike the monster - hold in L2 and move the right stick to focus over the stag. At the point when all is good and well, press square to free the bolt when the reticle becomes red. At the point when the monster falls, follow Atreus over to see him get done with the task.

Defeat Daudi Kaupmadr

As the savage connects with you, you'll observe that this foe is harder than the Draugr you've gone facing hitherto. This savage has a wellbeing bar so enormous it's contained two sets, and it will take a great deal of discipline to cut him down.

Note that when he assaults his chunk shines orange - this implies his hits are so large you will not have the option to obstruct them so don't attempt it.

All things being equal, center around avoid moving to the sides and circling back to a couple of cuts prior to withdrawing. You can utilize Atreus to occupy him by setting off him to fire bolts, and afterward assault when the savage's back is turned - Atreus is adequately deft to evade the assaults so don't stress over him.

The savage's assaults are normally a one-two punch: A low swinging push, trailed by an overhead hammer. Figure out how to peruse the development of these two assaults and trust that the hammer will begin assaulting with fast cuts or a couple of weighty assaults, then, at that point, ease off and begin throwing your hatchet or having Atreus shoot. In the event that you remain nearby too long the savage will thump you in reverse, making it harder to avoid the forthcoming assaults.

Subsequent to enduring many shots, the savage will begin switching around his assaults, and consolidate a wild swinging chain that fortunately doesn't have a tremendous reach, permitting you to reinforcement and substitute hatchet tosses and bow shots. Toward the finish of his swings you'll see him throw his weapon down and begin gasping - that is your signal to run over (press in on the left stick) and begin assaulting until he recovers his endurance. On the off chance that you begin getting low on wellbeing, draw him into separating stone squares and you may discover some wellbeing inside.

Continue to battle warily and don't get excessively ravenous with hits or excessively delayed with your avoiding. Try not to be hesitant to allow Atreus to take a portion of the hotness while you set up your next series of assaults. When the savage's wellbeing is drained, press in on the right stick when provoked to polish the beast off for great.

Get back to the House

With the chase settled, it's an ideal opportunity to head home. Search for a sparkling divider to help Atreus up and afterward follow him on the way. More Draugr will show up here, and you'll have the option to evaluate completing moves by raising a foe's shock meter.

The paralyze meter raises when foes are assaulted one after another - however raise at an exceptionally quick rate when immediately hit with Kratos' uncovered clench hands or Atreus' bolts. You can likewise cause a great deal of paralyze harm by utilizing weighty assaults to thump foes into the conditions - like into trees or dividers. Once dazed, you'll see a brief to snatch and kill them by squeezing R3. On account of more grounded foes with various wellbeing bar sets, you can in a split second drain one of the bars by utilizing the completing assault.

After the fight, you can recognize an enormous entryway ahead, however it's fixed with a frosty blue square that Kratos can't as yet open. This is a Hidden Chamber, and the locks must be opened by specific implies that you don't yet have. Fortunately, it will be set apart on your guide so you will not fail to remember its area when you really do acquire that capacity.

Move up the incline on the left to observe more Draugr pausing. Utilize the shock meter to complete adversaries rapidly by smacking them into dividers. In the end, a blue adversary will arise, some sort of Reaver.

This frigid adversary appears to be generally invulnerable to the Leviathan Ax - however fortunately your clench hands can do the work. It can likewise attempt to freeze you, and will go ballistic assuming it detects you are dialed back and frozen. Lay into the animal and don't ease up until you can pull off a finisher - and remember to utilize Atreus to pile up the shock harm.

With these beasts killed, you can now break the symbol obstructing the plummet down to the house. Atreus will run inside, and you can go along with him for a scene before things begin to change.

Rout the Stranger
At the point when this new baffling enemy shows up, you will need to watch out. This adversary has different wellbeing bars and seems somewhat erratic.

He'll give you the main hit, however at that point promptly begin running around to rapidly thrust at you with mind boggling pace and power. Fortunately you can impede these assaults, and obstructing at the perfect time will even bear the cost of you a countering blow.

Depend on fast evades and squares, and afterward attempt and get him in the air with a weighty strike prior to hanging a combo of lighter strikes together. You can likewise weighty strike him into trees to bargain extra harm.

At the point when he hops back, he might attempt to yell to send a quake of ice your direction - yet realize that you can shock him before he sends it by tossing your hatchet at his face.

Assault rapidly and be prepared for any of his running strikes until you can trim his wellbeing down to around two bars. Now he'll thump you onto the top of the house, yet when you get on top, begin smacking him as quick as possible before he can counter. Tragically, as the battle draws on, it becomes evident that this secret enemy may be simply impossible for you.

That is, until Spartan Rage kicks in.

Under the impacts of Spartan Rage, your assaults will be restored with force - you'll run towards your adversary at unimaginable speed and you can release a whirlwind of blows with the light assault. At the point when your rival takes a stab at avoiding aside or back to send up and an ice quake, utilize a weighty assault to jump out of sight and crash down managing harm in a wide region.

Keep up the offense however much you can until the Spartan Rage at last wears off. You'll have to drain his wellbeing down to around one bar this time, so be prepared to counter him.

Assuming he begins a combo on you, be prepared with the safeguard to hinder and send him flying, then, at that point, race towards him to keep up the hostile, possibly waiting to paralyze or throw you hatchet assuming he takes a stab at sending along quakes at you.

When you get him down far enough Kratos will bring the aggravation down on this foe, yet even that won't stop him for eternity. As the battle seethes on, you'll ultimately be thrown down a bluff, and need to scale the precipice as the more interesting insults you. At the point when you get up, you'll be thrown back to the opposite side of the canyon for a last session.

His assaults will come similarly as they did previously, yet he'll evade to the side significantly more to set up a combo (which you can counter with a very much planned safeguard block), and he'll likewise jump high up and crash down where your position is.

When he's up, race to the side then, at that point, pivot - and when he hits the ground, run over and release on him. Continue to do this example, and be prepared to move in the event that he begins to project his ice quakes.

At the point when you at last exhaust his wellbeing one final time, you'll have the option to end the battle. All that is left is to make the sluggish trip back to the house and get Atreus, then, at that point, the excursion to the mountain may really start.

PATH TO THE MOUNTAIN

Journey to the Mountain

As you start your excursion through the recently made crevice from your battle with the Stranger, make certain to survey your abilities. The experience you gain from finishing excursions and killing adversaries can be generally used to buy new abilities - however some require your hatchet to be worked on first. Consider getting a nearby battle ability for your hatchet, just as redesigning Atreus' battle abilities, as he'll be along for the whole ride - and is significantly more valuable than you anticipate.

Head down the gorge and shimmy across the edge until you arrive at a hole you can bounce across. On the opposite side, search for markings on a stone divider that you can climb, and afterward cross up to one side prior to panning further right to jump the remainder of the way to a high edge.

The passage here prompts an old mining cave - and you'll have to track down a way up. Gather the close by bunches of Hacksilver, and examine the extreme ideal for a pail you can wreck to get more Hacksilver. Atreus will make reference to helping him up on an edge close to the right half of the cave. Once up, he can't proceed ahead, yet there is an extension you can lower. Look behind you for a wheel you can turn to bring down the extension, then, at that point, freeze the stuff set up so Atreus can cross.

Order Atreus to drop the chain permitting you to scale, and by keeping the extension frozen you can cross to a stamped divider. Before you do that, turn the alternate method for coming up short on an edge where you can recognize a far off chest.

Jump across the edges to arrive at it and guarantee the Hacksilver Chest, then, at that point, return across the extension and get your hatchet back prior to ascending and bouncing to different edges up and afterward left to another stage. Here you can bring down one more chain for a more straightforward time frame backtracking later.

Proceed up the following divider until you arrive at the top, and respect the perspective on your old home prior to progressing forward. As you run up the following way and steer through a thin pass, you'll end up in the following region: The Riverpass.

As you enter, snatch some Hacksilver from a body as an afterthought as you approach more Draugr.

Time your attack with Atreus' bolts to develop combos on your foes rapidly or raise their stagger meter. Subsequent to felling a couple of Draugr, others will give the idea that fire shots. Convey note of your intimidation pointer - when the purple bolt erupts, you're going to be assaulted from a far distance.

Fortunately your safeguard can impede their blows - and you can then toss your hatchet at those pestering you from far off or have Atreus assist with trimming them down.

When this region is clear, gaze upward above to recognize a couple of pails of Hacksilver, and snatch the healthstone in the corner under the fallen tree assuming you want it. The exit plan lies by a few fascinating looking runes by a stone divider

Lore Location:

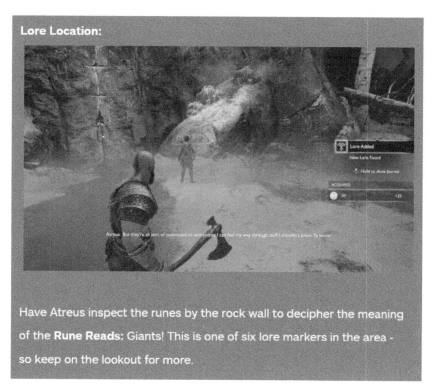

Have Atreus inspect the runes by the rock wall to decipher the meaning of the **Rune Reads:** Giants! This is one of six lore markers in the area - so keep on the lookout for more.

Proceed Towards the Mountain

Climb the stone divider in the wake of perusing the runes and snatch some Hacksilver from a cadaver on the left prior to moving onwards. Another blue frigid champion will snare you here - stay away from their ice assaults and pound them with your clench hands and bolts to end the battle rapidly.

You'll before long have the chance to test it out - as arriving at the following region will before long make them fall into ruins loaded up with Draugr that enliven to life.

Not every one of them will wake up immediately, so rush to take out the ones nearest and use Atreus to assist with swarming control - and use your Runic Attack when confronting a few of them nearby. A few shot tossing Draugr will show up on an edge above - remember your marker as you take out the nearer dangers prior to throwing your hatchet above to polish off the remainder of the aggressors.

Legendary Chest Location:

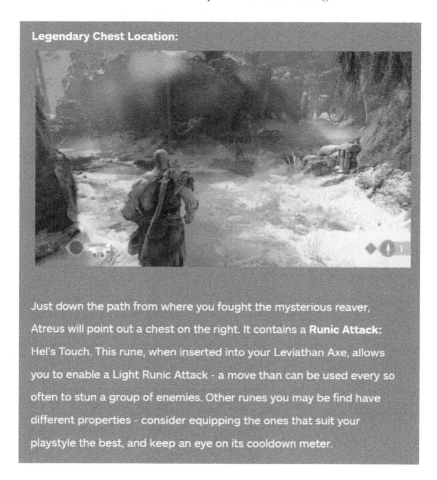

Just down the path from where you fought the mysterious reaver, Atreus will point out a chest on the right. It contains a **Runic Attack: Hel's Touch**. This rune, when inserted into your Leviathan Axe, allows you to enable a Light Runic Attack - a move than can be used every so often to stun a group of enemies. Other runes you may be find have different properties - consider equipping the ones that suit your playstyle the best, and keep an eye on its cooldown meter.

Get away from the Ruins

These foes are a lot harder than the normal Draugr. They sport two separate wellbeing bars that should be trimmed down, and assault with weighty tomahawks that can overwhelm your safeguard or by and large slice through it - assuming you see a yellow light exude from their assault, prepare to evade aside, as impeding these will stun you significantly. They will typically perform a couple of these unblockable assaults, or a more modest hatchet push that can be obstructed at the ideal opportunity.

Recall that structure up a stagger meter on these enemies can permit you to totally clear out one of the wellbeing bars and genuinely harm them - simply don't get encircled. You additionally reasonable have a stocked bar of fury to actuate your Spartan Rage: like your battle with the Stranger, this permits you to bargain a great deal of harm in a short measure of time, and hit foes so hard they may very well fly into dividers or off the close by bluff.

Contend energetically and cautious, and use Atreus at whatever point conceivable to occupy the foes until all the Heavy Draugr are dead. Presently you can climb another divider where they got through and head further into the vestiges.

As you move up the divider, you'll hear some truly frightening reciting. Tread carefully, and make certain to fall to pieces a few wooden boards on the right as you drop down to get some Hacksilver by a cadaver. There's one more carcass with more Hacksilver up on the left behind more wooden boards. Try not to stress over the dead Draugr, they aren't making the commotions. As you enter the bigger stage, a Revenant will show up.

These witches are tricky and send poison fog your direction or with swipes of their staff - however the genuine irritation comes from their steady magically transport evading.

They'll dodge you pretty much without fail, except if you use Atreus and his bolts to stagger them long enough for you to run up and begin smacking them around. Look out for a counter assault, and afterward sit tight for them to magically transport again prior to telling more bolt salvos.

In the wake of overcoming the Revenant, head through the passage under the scaffold to a hole with a far divider you can leap to and climb.

Nonetheless, assuming that you need some fortune, move down first. At the base you can enter the pit underneath the area you were first in.

Sadly, a level 3 Heavy Draugr will seem to do fight - and it's actual intense. It might utilize similar moves, yet its assaults are inside and out unblockable, and even its short punch can stun you in the event that you attempt and square it. Battle cautiously and use your Runic capacity to paralyze it and have Atreus continue to pepper away at the beast until you can kill it. Your prize are two cans over the pit loaded with Hacksilver, and a huge Coffin containing more Hacksilver, just as Aegir's Gold and Soft Svartalheim Steel - parts you'll require for improving stuff.

Head back to the tall stone divider and move up to the top where you can detect your objective past a fixed entryway. Head right first to open up another enormous Coffin that contains a Soft Svartalheim Steel. Hop across the hole yet be prepared for a trap by Draugr, with more showing up down on the way to one side.

Odin's Ravens Location:

From where you took out the projectile-throwing Draugr, look just above along the ridge to spot a glowing green raven. This is one of Odin's Ravens, the eyes and ears of the god himself. Throw your axe at it to destroy it, and you'll earn some experience for the task.

At long last, move up the short edge in this passed on way region to observe a body holding a stone shining various shadings. Break the stone when it is red to recuperate all fury, green to recuperate all wellbeing, or white to acquire 25 XP! You can likewise find a chest close by with more Hacksilver.

With the left way investigated, it's an ideal opportunity to head right.

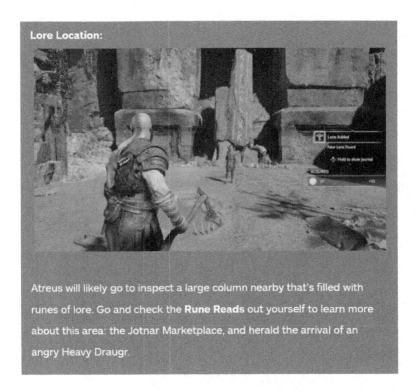

Lore Location:

Atreus will likely go to inspect a large column nearby that's filled with runes of lore. Go and check the **Rune Reads** out yourself to learn more about this area: the Jotnar Marketplace, and herald the arrival of an angry Heavy Draugr.

Recross the scaffold and look into ideal for an edge prompting a Hacksilver Chest. As you forge ahead to where the frigid blue enemy assaulted - prepare for one more enormous conflict in this huge region, as different sorts of Draugr and a Revenant will all assault without a moment's delay.

Ensure you kill the Revenant first - you might even need to release Spartan Rage once you're certain Atreus has paralyzed it, then, at that point, center around drawing the Heavy Draugr away from the shot tossing Draugr, so you can run back and dispense with them, leaving the heavies for last.

With these adversaries disposed of, raise the scaffold down a piece by utilizing the close by wheel until you see the chain down on the left, and hold it set up while you obliterate the seal to wrap up wrecking the extension.

Cross, and look right to observe a Coffin holding Soft Svartalfheim Steel.

Note the heaps of dead bodies as you gravitate toward the following door - it's reasonable they weren't put here for beautification. On the opposite side, you'll be trapped by frenzied people - human Reavers.

Fortunately, these folks are a weakling, and a solitary runic impact will nearly kill every one of them close by. When you polish them off, watch for mages that appear on the overhangs and take them out with hatchet tosses.

After the following scene, you'll track down what were once Reavers are currently turning into the frosty blue adversaries you battled before. Abandon your hatchet and begin beating - or utilize Spartan Rage to steer the results in support of yourself. However long you use your clench hands, they won't keep going long.

After the fight, send Atreus up the divider to bring down the chain for you - however he'll be justifiably furious about late occasions, so make certain to persuade him alongside orders until he gets to the chain to get you up. Move up, and abandon the remnants.

Proceed Towards the Mountain
Outside the remnants, shimmy across the edge, and you'll observe yourself to be high over the commercial center that you fell into before. On the off chance that you missed it previously, one of Odin's Ravens will be roosted on a close by edge. Make certain to look right to observe a major Coffin holding Soft Svartalfheim Steel, and afterward utilize the close by chain to drop down to a lower level.

Lore Locations:

After killing them, look along the right side of the left path to find a **Lore Scroll**: Svartalfheim Sealed, and have Atreus pick it up and read it.

Head further left to the end to find a **Jotnar Shrine** and open the cabinet to have Atreus take a look at it to reveal Hrungnir.

At this point you've presumably heard the calls of an exceptionally furious individual and the whimpers of a pack animal. Progress forward the fundamental way to an enormous stone scaffold to find the source: a Dwarf is attempting to get his pack creature across the extension.

At the idea of Atreus, toss your hatchet at the white trees across the scaffold, and things will move along to the Dwarven Shop of Brok. Here you can update existing hardware like the Leviathan Ax, and art totally new stuff like covering - assuming that you have the coin and fixings.

Start by taking the Frozen Flame that Brok has given you to overhaul the Leviathan Ax to even out 2. This will permit you to bargain more harm, yet buy better abilities utilizing the experience you've acquired. You can likewise make some protective layer - pick the Reaver Armor on the off chance that you're getting hit alot or the Boar Hide to bargain more harm.

Remember to overhaul Atreus' Talon Bow too - in addition to the fact that this gives him new abilities to buy, yet you can create unique protection for him too that can make him more valuable in either run offense, scuffle offense, or backing. Pick one that suits your playstyle the best, and open an expertise or two in the meantime. You ought to have to the point of creating one piece of protection for Kratos and Atreus, and overhaul his bow. Assuming you're short on Hacksilver, recall that you can sell the Artifacts you find for a nice sum - they fill no other need once gathered.

After this, you can scrutinize your new covering and weapons on a couple of Draugr that bring forth. Watch for the shot hurlers along the back as you dance around the Heavy Draugr. Take them out, and prepare to move out. You can get back to Brok's Shop at whatever point you want, however hope to observe more shops as you investigate.

Continue Through the Gate to the Mountain

Get back to the Dwarven Shop and move left past the entryway to observe a raised extension you can strike down. This leads down to the way sitting above the locked rune chest you saw as before, and you can at long last tear open the close by Hacksilver Chest. Hope to left to track down a chain to descend into that passage with the fixed door. Prior to going down the chain, pivot to observe a Raven you can toss your hatchet at. Presently continue to go down the chain and open up the huge Coffin for a Soft Svartalfheim Steel, and afterward open the far entryway for an easy route.

Get back to the principle entryway and said goodbye to Brok as you open the door involving the chain and freeze it set up while you enter. There's a comparable chain on the opposite side to return.

Creeping through the passage ahead, obviously this cavern is likely brimming with risks, what with the heaps of skeletons.

You'll before long show up at a steel spiked divider - not something Kratos can punch his direction through. Notwithstanding, there's a wooden board at the upper right you can toss your hatchet at to turn the steel spikes on its pivots.

At the following spike entryway, you'll need to toss it two times to shift it aside - yet note that it impedes a section prompting a Coffin. Toss your hatchet again to continue to shift the spikes to the side to arrive at it and snatch a Soft Svartalfheim Steel.

Up ahead, things seem truly dreadful: A spike pit isolates you from an imploded spiky roof. You can hit the raised board on the left to turn it and raise the roof, yet it will gradually bring down over the long haul - and you would rather not get found out under that.

Hit the board a couple of times and afterward freeze the square underneath the board to keep the roof set up - until further notice. As you bounce across, you'll be trapped by Draugr. Fight the temptation to get back to your hatchet and begin stepping them - assuming you send off them into spike dividers with weighty assaults they'll take huge harm and set themselves up for a finisher.

More Draugr will show up back across the pit, so jump back and snatch your hatchet on the off chance that you need or simply continue to punch until these new fortifications are no more. At long last, a Heavy Draugr will show up back under the spiky roof - you can allow him to get squashed assuming you're feeling shrewd, or run over and punch him into the spiky dividers.

When every one of the enemies are dead, keep the roof raised and investigate around. You might have broken a wooden hindrance in the battle that prompts a Hacksilver Chest. You can likewise recognize a locked chest above set apart with Runes, yet leave it for the present. To move beyond this area in one piece, you should be fast.

Remain close to the spike entryway and require your hatchet. Immediately hit it a couple of times to open a way, then, at that point, begin tossing your hatchet on the board to one side of the way to keep the roof raised, and refreeze it in a hurry. Once across, you can at last get back to your hatchet and released the roof down.

Artifact Location:

Dropping down the chain near the ruins exit, you can take the path to a ridge overlooking the Marketplace, and a ledge going back up to the entrance.

Near the ledge is a dead soldier holding one of The Faces of Magic masks, part of artifact set.

Presently you can at last forget about the cavern and head onto a little level that disregards the mountain somewhere out there. However, the street is yet well before you'll arrive at it.

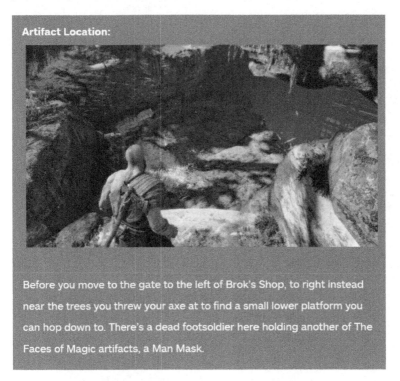

Artifact Location:

Before you move to the gate to the left of Brok's Shop, to right instead near the trees you threw your axe at to find a small lower platform you can hop down to. There's a dead footsoldier here holding another of The Faces of Magic artifacts, a Man Mask.

Head up the way towards a huge and forcing entry with two monster sculptures. As Atreus assesses the sand bowl in the middle, he'll interpret a question.

It is by all accounts connected with the goliath entrance and the rings that aren't moving. Glance around to one side to discover some Hacksilver close to a body and move up a close by edge to track down a component. This will begin moving the rings, head down to assess the riddle.

As it turns you can recognize a few uncovered cog wheels, and you can hit with your hatchet to stop portions of the ring, and pull the hatchet back when the following nearest ring coordinates. Hit the external one first, and hang tight for it to adjust to shape a "D" type rune toward the end. Presently hit the middle stuff, and hang tight for the entire line of runes to adjust prior to pulling your hatchet back, with "A" looking rune close to the "D" rune.

Have Atreus perused out the finished word, and the way forward will be uncovered.

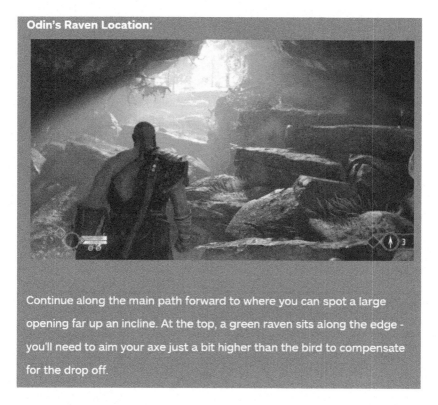

Odin's Raven Location:

Continue along the main path forward to where you can spot a large opening far up an incline. At the top, a green raven sits along the edge - you'll need to aim your axe just a bit higher than the bird to compensate for the drop off.

Chase with Atreus

As you leave the little cavern, you'll recognize a few tracks in the mud, and Atreus will start another chase after this secret monster.

This chase will be in a matter of seconds hindered by the appearance of another savage: Brenna Daudi. This beast is harder than the principal savage you battled, however you have new abilities and stuff available to you. This savage is additionally imbued with shoot, and will heave magma at you with its free hand, or make a monstrous step or weapon bang to spread discharge in a circle around it.

Wait when it does this and spotlight on went assaults, then, at that point, run in and assault when the way is clear. Evade the comparable punches and pummels it prefers the last Troll did, and use your runic assault to keep it shaky when it attempts to energize an assault.

Reaver Shadows will begin seeming to irritate you with poison shots - watch out for the field and run over to manage them, as they'll ordinarily be far enough away that you can kill them without stressing over the savage surprising you.

As he gets more angered, he'll bargain more fire assaults you really want to avoid - yet you can likewise utilize your Spartan Rage to keep the savage stupefied and hindered by your consistent assaults. When you can bargain sufficient harm, you'll have the option to polish off the savage for great in ruthless style.

Your compensation for this manager battle is another Heavy Runic Attack - Ivaldi's Anvil. Actuated similar as the light runic assault, this will cause a huge area of impact ice harm to hit loads of targets, which can be extraordinary with overpowered. You'll likewise get heaps of Hacksilver and some Soft Svartalfheim Steel from killing the beast, so make certain to get all the close by plunder.

Odin's Raven Location:

After defeating the troll, look up at the giant bony ribcage of some long dead giant thing to spot a glowing green raven perched on one of the middle ribs. Launch your axe it to kill it.

Make certain to check out the supervisor field for more plunder. Of on the right side assuming a little stage you can bounce up to observe a chest holding Hacksilver. Further right is a stream you can go to track down a dead body toward the end with more Hacksilver.

Idunn Apple Location:

Off to the left side of the arena is a cliff overlooking the distant mountain that is a **Nornir Chest** locked by three runic seals. The "N" looking rune is found just behind it - but it can't be broken. When it stops ringing, the seal will reappear so you need to be quick to find the others.

The "R" looking rune is found just to the left above the waterfall.

The "C" looking rune is located back upstream behind one of the giant ribs. Hit them all quickly and you'll unlock the Nornir Chest to gain the third Idunn Apple and increase your health.

To forge ahead, search for a light almost a little cavern and pass through - halting to get some Hacksilver from a dead fighter. On the opposite side of the cavern you can detect the pig Atreus is chasing down beneath. Drop down, and climb behind Atreus as he readies his bow.

Like the stag, you'll have to delicately direct Atreus to his imprint, Hold in the L2 and point until the marker becomes red and afterward press square. It may not go as arranged, however the chase should continue.

As you drop down to follow the hog, you'll wind up at the foot of a destroyed town - something awful occurred here.

The town is by all accounts site of a fight among Reavers and Draugr - yet it appears as though you can grab the plunder.

Look on the stage you hopped down from for a powerless wooden divider to break, and plunder the Hacksilver Chest. The close by cabin on the right additionally conceals some Hacksilver - simply separate the way to give yourself access. There's one more open house a couple of entryways down with more Hacksilver inside.

As you advance toward the solitary hovel further down the way, seek the left for an edge you can scale where a Hacksilver Chest is, just as a pail hanging above you can wreck.

Be careful as you approach the last cabin, as one of the blue-reavers will leap out to trap you. Bludgeon him into the side of the structure to shock and take him out rapidly, then, at that point, snatch some Hacksilver inside.

Atreus will follow the hog under a monster point of support, and this time he'll make the following effort without help from anyone else. After an effective hit, he'll pursue the pig down the hazy way, passing on you to follow and track down your delinquent child.

Track down Atreus
As the mist wraps you, you'll enter a limited labyrinth of ways, and should depend on calling out for Atreus to push ahead. Move right at the principal fork, and afterward bring the main left down a section.

Race to the following light and shout to hear him call from the right. Follow the way as it twists through a cavern to the opposite side, finishing off with one more crossroads. Head left and continue to climb until you vault over a little snag and through a tight hole into the following region.

At the point when you show up, you'll be provoked to utilize both L2 and R2 to assist in an errand, prior to worrying about your concern and moving onwards.

Follow the Witch
Start your slow stroll into the Sanctuary Grove. There's no risk here - it's a secured region similar as your house was up to this point. Toward the finish of the way you'll be welcomed inside a house, so continue to move.

Once inside, you're next errand will be to discover a few white-petaled blossoms. Leave out the indirect access and into the nursery.

The external opens up to an enormous stream, with a way to the left and right. You can walk right to address Atreus assuming that you need, yet assuming that you're looking for the blossoms, head left towards a stone segment and check out it to assemble the blossoms.

Get once again to the opposite side of the nursery and assist Atreus with get-together his plants by giving him back his blade. Presently you can get back to the home with the two fixings.

After a couple of scenes, you'll be on your way once more, taking an exit through the Witch's Cave. You'll likewise acquire another thing - the Witches Compass. It will follow your primary target at the highest point of your HUD (But you can switch it off in the settings assuming you don't need the interruption).

Head down through the cavern to a fundamental stage just to be trapped by Nightmares. These flying animals are really delicate however dart around and shoot poison shots. Block them with your safeguard and fight back by tossing your hatchet or having Atreus hit them.

From the primary stage, there's secrets flourish - however not every one of them can be tackled presently. A sparkling red entryway ahead can't be open at this time, and a gleaming entryway further beyond a cascade lies far off.

You can head left down a little way with a body holding Hacksilver, down to the waterfront where a Draugr and his un-vivified companion are. There's a ton down in the water, however Kratos isn't one for swimming. You can anyway pivot to observe a major pile of stone chunks on a lift that Kratos can pull over towards the water.

Pull to the side until you can't move it any farther and let go, then, at that point, look behind the stack to observe a Coffin containing Soft Svartalfheim Steel.

Since the leftover secrets should hang tight for one more day, head back up to the fundamental stage and bounce across the stone stages toward the boat,

Boat Towards Daylight

Since you've done everything you can in the cavern, head down to the harbors and get on the boat to see yourself out of the cavern. Once in the water, continue heading through the winding passage (you can dock at genuine docks) until you come out to see the far off mountain.

Going through the following passage, you'll at last wind up out onto an extraordinary lake - the Shores of Nine, named for the incomparable Lake of Nine. Sculptures of Norse Gods litter this place...as accomplishes something different.

Atreus will bring up a sparkling sculpture close to the focal point of the lake, so paddle on over to research.

When the scene here closes, you'll at long last get a decent glance at the Lake of Nine - and this spot truly opens up. The changing water level has uncovered loads of side regions to investigate and side missions to attempt, which you can begin doing now. Note that a considerable lot of these areas might have specific hindrances to impede your development until you have the right instruments or capacities, this incorporates getting back to the Witch's Cave.

To investigate another region, search for the white banners that signify moor areas or low shores to push the boat to ground. To get more data about these secret regions, see the rundown beneath:

Post Tower, situated on the South finish of the lake close to the Witch's Cave.

Muspelheim Tower, found in the South on the opposite side of the entry to the Witch's cavern.

Niflheim Tower, situated on the inward ring of the Southwest side of the Lake.

Iron Cove, found in the far Southwest region of the Lake past Niflheim Tower.

Isle of Death, a little broken island stage found in the West, only North of Iron Cove.

Neglected Caverns, situated in the internal ring of the Northwest side of the lake between the snake's body.

Helheim Tower, found on the North finish of the Lake close to some portion of the snake's body.

Alfheim Tower, situated on the internal ring of the Northeast piece of the Lake, situated by a goliath fixed entryway.

Stone Falls, found to the furthest East of the Lake past the Alfheim Tower. This area likewise has a wheel component that opens the close by brilliant entryway to a secret district: Veithurgard.

Volunder Mines, situated in the far Southeast region of the Lake past the frigid entry past the Cliffs of the Raven.

Precipices of the Raven, found in the South and part of the lake on the East side, near Vanaheim Tower.

Vanaheim Tower, situated on the South side of the lake near the entry to Lookout Tower.

Explore the Temple and Bridge

Mooring the boat on the middle island of Tyr's Temple, you can land on one or the other side under an enormous extension. As you come up to the top, the wonderful sight of the mountain will be hindered by the arrival of a close buddy, who has obviously settled in inside the actual sanctuary.

Inside the sanctuary, converse with Brok and he'll provide you with a stone of the World Tree. Utilizing it, you can open up gateways in various areas to use as a quick travel gadget - yet you want to think that they are first.

Brok likewise has significantly more available to be purchased, including new protection, charms, hatchet handle, improvements, and redesigns for things like Atreus' bolt shudder. Make certain to furnish Kratos in a full suit of new stuff and handle, and overhaul on the off chance that you have cash to save - and buy another ability or two assuming you are capable.

Note that any ancient rarities you offer to Brok will really wind up in plain view, just as selling for a lot of Hacksilver - gather them all!

Advance toward the Tower

Moving along the long scaffold you can track down a middle stage with a system that ascents up to a huge horn - in any case, Kratos isn't going to blow on monster horns without knowing what it may do.

Back down on the extension, cross to the Vanaheim Tower where you'll be trapped by harmed Reavers. They are not really men any longer, and keeping in mind that they might pass on simple, they'll detonate upon death and expect you to withdraw except if you need to be killed. On the in addition to side, Atreus has become sure to the point of utilizing more skirmish assaults and his abilities will have grown to some degree.

Outside the pinnacle, you can plunder two chests for Hacksilver, and there are a few close by engravings that Artreus can't unravel at this time. At the point when you're prepared to head in, go to the entryway and open it.

Go Through the Tower and Caves

Within the pinnacle more Reavers are battling a Tatzelwurm, and will then, at that point, go to battle you. If their propensity to detonate is irritating you, you can take a stab at freezing them with specific assaults to balance this, as they won't pass on when killed while frozen.

Since Atreus can't peruse different markers in the primary lobby, go right to observe your direction hindered by poison. The Scorn Pole is the wellspring of this toxic substance, and you can freeze it by tossing your hatchet at the shining post.

Get the Hacksilver from the dead bodies uncovered by the shortfall of toxin and afterward move to one side past the shaft to another post you really want to freeze, and follow the way to a sinkhole with stages going down. Look above and thump down a container of Hacksilver prior to dropping down yourself.

As you eliminate the following Scorn Pole from play, the Tatzelwurm that was battling the Reavers before will jump out of the ground to assault. It jumps at the chance to tunnel around far away prior to thrusting to assault, however assuming you time it right you can without much of a stretch square or avoid far removed and circle back to staggering assaults to manage it before it can hit you with its toxin thorn.

Since you can't connect with the close by legend marker, move up the divider by the Scorn Pole and bounce across to the opposite side of the cavern where another entryway is standing by.

On the opposite side of the entryway you'll enter the locale known as the Foothills, and encounter another Dwarf, and with it, another shop! Sindri will vow to upgrade your stuff decently well, so it merits looking at his shop just as Brok's now and again.

The shop presently sells Resurrection Stones, things you can convey that let Atreus bring Kratos back from death during an extreme battle. They are single use, and you can convey one at time, yet it's incredibly helpful while wandering into the unexplored world.

Proceed Towards the Mountain
Abandoning Sindri, head up into the Foothills.

On the right you'll observe a final resting place encompassed by poison that you can't reach from the start - however look behind the stones and you can see a Scorn Pole to scatter it, permitting you to plunder an Arcane Waist Guard, just as some Hacksilver by a dead body. Moving left beyond an odd instrument you'll track down a pail in the trees with Hacksilver, and past it a locked chest.

Further passed on just prompts two Coffins that can't as of now be opened with your apparatuses, so head up the center way to a Hacksilver Chest, and search for a stone divider you can move to a higher stage.

As you take out the first of the Scorn Poles, a Revenant will show up prior to running back up the way - don't get hurried and gone through more Scorn Poles.

All things considered, let her escape and follow the left way rather past one more Scorn Pole to a region with some Hacksilver on the ground and a Coffin hindered by a close by Scorn Pole you can disseminate to get Arcane Bracers - wrist covering that increment your Cooldown.

Back on the way clear out the following Scorn Pole and get the Revenant back into public. Have Atreus continue to daze as you give pursue, and be prepared to get your hatchet back and get out other Scorn Poles as the foe retreats into other noxious regions.

Assuming you follow the correct way in the wake of killing the Revenant, you'll enter little cavern prompting another puzzling locked entryway - the Hidden Chamber of Odin. Likewise with the Wildwoods, you can't open it now, yet a guide marker will be added so you can return when the opportunity arrives.

Follow the left way past the draping Scorn Pole to a high divider you can move up to an enormous stage.

Here, more debased Ravagers stand by alongside Poison Wolves - who will heave poison gunk on the ground before them. Trim them down from a remote place then, at that point, avoid around them when they come to assault and take them out before you get harmed.

Be aware of this area you investigate - there are hazardous urns all over, and hitting one will explode the region around it, yet additionally dispose of neighboring rubble. You can involve this on the urn in the back left to uncover a secret Coffin holding Arcane Shoulder Wraps and Soft Svartalfheim Steel.

Leave the remainder of the urns alone as you head towards the entryway toward the end - and you'll be hindered by another foe - the Ogre, just as more Reavers coming up behind you.

The Ogre is exceptionally scary, and it utilizes both unblockable charge assaults and strong hammers or swinging arms that will stun you assuming you don't impede at the exact second. It can (and typically will) run over to a close by Reaver and throw the foe right at you assuming that you're not focusing. It's to your greatest advantage to run around the field, freezing Reavers and taking them out so they don't detonate, and tossing your hatchet at them assuming you see them raise their arms to mend.

Assuming you have Spartan Rage dynamic, have a go at developing a great deal of daze on the Ogre and you'll have the option to bargain a ton of harm just as ride the beast around and use it to crush into the Reavers.

Once back on the ground, be careful about its turning clench hands and use your Runic capacities to keep it reeling when you can. Assuming that you let a few urns be, you can likewise utilize them for your potential benefit assuming you can bait adversaries close prior to exploding them - simply be cautious it doesn't backfire.

At the point when the Ogre goes down, you can forge ahead your way subsequent to plundering it for a Symbol of Truth Enchantment, 5 Soft Svartalfheim Steel, and a Frozen Flame (used to overhaul your hatchet!).

Entering through the goliath entryway, you'll end up at the Mountain's Base. There's a genuinely slick goliath face cut solidly into the side of the mountain you can respect as you gaze toward the move in front of you.

Disregard the casket hindered by the blue roots and continue to climb the mountain way to where the monster face in the stone is by all accounts heaving smoke. You can get some Hacksilver to one side of the principle way and spot one more chest shrouded in those blue roots.

As you arrive at the Black Breath, you'll observe that it's blocked - however the appearance of a companion might give the resources to avoid this dim enchantment.

A REALM BEYOND

Follow the Witch

With the way up the mountain obstructed for the occasion, you really want another option, and it might lie past the domain of Midgard.

First of all - follow your partner back to Sindri's skymover and watch it sort out, permitting you to sidestep journeying down the Foothills to where Sindri's Shop was.

Head to the entryway back through the cavern and sanctuary, and you'll observe that your companion has a few stunts to get across holes and closed down Scorn Poles...hopefully you'll get a portion of that power for yourself soon.

As you leave the pinnacle, you'll look into the world - including what those insane undead blue folks are called, and your companion will request that you head down the steps on your left side toward the dock - and afterward turn right.

Realign the Bridge

As the way forward is made for you, you must fix up the harm to Tyr's Temple. Search for a huge broken and broadened hub past the new extension you crossed and set up it back.

You can now push the pivot to move the whole sanctuary island and scaffold to highlight another pinnacle. Continue to push until the extension focuses toward the East, and afterward return up top.

Presently you can enter the sanctuary (Brok is by all accounts enjoying some time off and certainly wouldn't fret) and another scaffold will be reached out to the focal point of the sanctuary. Atreus bow will before long be captivated with a similar capacity to make these scaffolds - yet solely after you have gotten the Light of Alfheim in the following domain.

Go to Alfheim

Once through the nearby, you'll end up in the Realm Traversal Room. Follow your partner to the middle where the foundations of the World Tree encompass a stage in an obscured room, and head around the back to review a platform.

As you watch, the stage will transform into a guide of the Shore of Nine, showing the sanctuary and the domain that the scaffold prompts - the domain you wish to enter. Right now you're pointed at Vanaheim, however Odin has forestalled travel to this domain. All things being equal, turn the wheel to Alfheim. When you select it, you'll be given the Travel Rune expected to get to this domain. Lock in your objective and the Bifrost will actuate, zeroing in on the blue gem that will send you to this new domain.

It may not appear as though you've gone anyplace - yet looks can be deluding, as the various domains are both the same and dissimilar to.

As you leave the sanctuary, you'll see exactly the way that various things are. You can likewise detect the Light of Alfheim somewhere far off - however it gives off an impression of being blurring, which can't be great. Before your companion leaves, you'll be cautioned that the Bifrost is out of juice, and should be renewed with the Light of Alfheim...but another notice is interfered. You're on your own now - best be careful of the risks ahead.

THE LIGHT OF ALFHEIM

Find a Way to the Light

As you advance down the extension, you'll obviously acknowledge while certain parts of this area appear to be like Midgard, you won't observe anything you've abandoned in that domain. New fortunes and fear the same anticipate in this domain.

The domain of the light mythical beings is brimming with trees and forests, just as odd pink roots that block your way - however you can toss your hatchet at the throbbing mass in the middle to give entry. At the following blockage, admire the option to recognize an occupant of this world, the clear light mythical beings, secured human battle with the winged dull mythical beings. The bodies around you highlight a conflict being pursued even presently.

Just to one side of the runes, obliterate the pink roots to uncover a Hacksilver Chest.

Up ahead you'll detect a Light Elf, however it will before long be killed as a few Dark Elves show up, and you end up being in an unlucky spot.

Dull Elves dance around on their wings before plunge bombarding with their lances in a two hit combo or one in number hit, or shooting blazing pillars a ways off. You can keep one out of the battle by freezing it with a hatchet toss, or use your runic capacities to keep them reeling. Avoid weighty assaults that send off them very high, as you will not have the option to shuffle them adequately because of their wings - they'll simply fly and retreat - except if you freeze them first.

These foes can likewise hinder assaults, requiring solid assaults or the safeguard break update to push through to harm them. Ensure Atreus is assisting either by diverting them with his scuffle assaults and gags or peppering bolts to occupy them.

In the wake of killing the triplet, head up to track down more pink roots - and note that obliterating one of the throbbing centers adequately isn't - you want to arrange them so you can strike both on the double to get rid of the blockage for great.

Head down the way to the ocean side region to observe Sindri and another shop he's set up. Purchase or update assuming that you want to - he has new things to sell - and think about purchasing or redesigning some stuff to reach or draw near to even out 2. Foes are beginning to get intense, and you'll need to keep up. Recollect that overhauled stuff can be socketed with charms that can additionally help your abilities, and you have a Frozen Flame from killing the Ogre to update your Leviathan Ax to even out 3!

In the wake of talking with Sindri, pivot to detect a boat tangled in certain roots. Move along to the right side so you can arrange every one of the three throbbing centers and hit them with one toss, then, at that point, move the boat onto the water.

Get to the Ringed Temple
Note: It's barely noticeable, yet watch out for a low hanging sparkling blue dew swinging from a branch along the water. Have Atreus pluck it to observe the Yggdrasil's Dew of Cooldown, a uninvolved thing that will forever expand your Cooldown by 2.

As you paddle through the tight stream you'll come to the area known as the Lake of Light.

This spot, similar as the Shore of Nine, is home to a few more modest side experiences would it be advisable for you decide to share - yet be careful about risk. Toward the Southeast lies the Light Elf Sanctuary, and to the far West is the Light Elf Shore - the two spots you can dock at. There's additionally a sand bowl close to the entry to the lake that represents another question - however there are no runes present to assist you with tracking down the response yet.

Moving forward to the Ringed Temple, you can moor your boat and way to deal with observe the light extension fixed away by attaches that transition to cover the precious stone.

The Dark Elves will before long trap you in a bigger gathering. Try not to frenzy, and attempt to zero in on one and paralyze the others to break their development. Utilize Atreus to assist with culling them out of the air, or use your hatchet toss to dial them back - on the off chance that they are not moving around something over the top.

After they get taken out, you'll observe that you can't drop down from here - yet there are two wheel systems close to the dock. Pulling on them will uncover huge runes that surface out of the water - runes that may be utilized for the sand bowl back close to the lake entrance.

Take out the Dark Elf fortifications and return to the boat moving back to the lake entrance where the sand bowl enigma is. Since you can see the runes, Atreus can choose the response, uncovering a huge channel in the lake driving down to the sanctuary profundities.

As you enter the Ringed Temple Trench, more Dark Elves will come at you from all sides.

Simple Rage can assist with evening the chances here as you wallop them and smack them around to ward them from taking off. Ensure you freeze them when you can so they can't avoid around as fast, and use your Runic Abilities at whatever point they are dynamic to whittle down their groups.

Reactivate the Ringed Temple Bridge
When the region is clear, glance around to recognize a few hanging cases attached to those pink roots you can hit to get some Hacksilver. Behind you are two unique rooms loaded with confined Draugr and a system in the room.

Proceed down the principle way towards the sanctuary just to observe a goliath gap hindering your development. You'll have to figure out how to cross - and it might include going down.

Utilize the wheel instrument to drop the stages down as far as possible and you'll see a restricted section going inside the external sanctuary. Freeze the stuff while you run inside to another jail like region. There's one more wheel system here so you can return back outside - take a stab at utilizing it and you'll see a secret final resting place that is simply in the divider you can bring down a digit to your level, and afterward toss your hatchet at the stuff on the right. Head down the entry to open the Coffin and you'll get a Rare Enchantment - a Fragmented Heart of Alfheim. It lessens all harm from Dark Elves' assaults by 12% and is VERY helpful around here, so put it to utilize!

Head through the jail (there doesn't appear to be any method for opening the cells with the Draugr yet) into a room with two root centers you can point to hit both immediately. As you move out, you'll be trapped by a major appalling Dark Elf and his Dark Elf Warriors.

Now, you'll briefly lose both your hatchet and Atreus - however Kratos has fury to save. To such an extent that in the accompanying battle, you'll have limitless Spartan Rage, so burn through no time killing each Dark Elf that comes your direction.

At the point when the nearest adversaries have been managed, you'll have to track down a way to the far stage. Seek the appropriate for a huge divider and begin pounding it until you can quickly tap Circle to make a stage over to the center.

Since you have back with you, you'll be facing a large group of Dark Elf Warriors. These folks are more reinforced than the others you've battled, and move quicker to accuse their spear of running assaults that can break your watchman and cause shockwaves regardless of whether they miss hitting you straightforwardly. The assaults can likewise visually impaired and obscure your vision - which can make following their development an aggravation. Attempt and freeze one with a hatchet throw and afterward beatdown the other with Atreus utilizing his bolts to develop daze before it can take off to kill them rapidly.

After the two champions go down, you may see a close by chest enveloped by roots. Search for a little way going down the contrary side to a dead mythical person holding Hacksilver.

Look under the scaffold to one side to recognize one of two throbbing habitats - the other is under the chest, and you can bend the shot to hit both simultaneously. Presently you can return up to the primary stage and open the Coffin to get 1 Soft Svartalfheim Steel.

Since the vitally two pathways needs the light of Alfheim to cross, search for an entryway on the opposite side of the stage from the chest and enter through there. Inside is another jail like region with more Draugr in a correctional facility, and an idle lift in the center. Exit through the entryway on the right to a bigger region with a way beneath.

Down here, you'll have to remove the roots so the Light of Alfheim can leak through and power up a scaffold. Cross to the opposite side and move up where more Dark Elves will snare you.

Be on alarm for one waiting by an overhang attempting to kill you - you can install a hatchet in his face, and tear it out when he attempts to set up one more run impact.

As you kill them, you'll incidentally stir an Ancient - a being made of stone and components that truly needs you dead.

To kill it, you'll have to hit the flimsy spot that it ousts its essential assaults from - which can get dangerous as you'll have to avoid the shafts first. On the off chance that you hit its delicious focus, it will oust circles onto the ground. After you wrap up avoiding its impact, snatch a circle and throw it back to explode to unstable impact, further uncovering the flimsy spot to assault.

Keep this procedure up and you'll have the option to shock it genuinely quick, allowing you to get on top to bargain extra harm until you are misled. A few Dark Elf Warriors will before long join the battle - utilize the monster rock in the center as cover as you bait the mythical people to you can dispose of them so you can zero in back on the natural and rehash the method involved with staggering it until the animal falls.

Note that killing an Ancient will give you some extraordinary plunder - including another Dark Elf Enchantment (they stack!) and the Ancient's Heart - which you can exchange with the Dwarves to create the Ancient's Armor.

Presently that no doubt about it "root" of the issue, it's an ideal opportunity to get out this gunk that is hindering the fundamental extension into the internal sanctuary. Toss your hatchet to dispose of the defensive layer, then, at that point, go very close and charge your hatchet into the center to detonate it. This will get every one of the scaffolds this room back internet, permitting you a simpler method for returning to the top.

Enter the Temple
Head across the new extension back to the jail space to find the lift now completely functional, which will take you back up the pit you saw at the

scaffold entrance prior. Presently you can cross the extension and enter the blue entryway into the Ringed Temple appropriate... yet the entryway doesn't appear to have where you can open it. Oopsies.

Track down Another Way Into the Temple

Head down the other way to catch Sindri once more. Since you have the Ancient's Heart, he'll have the option to grow new creating plans to make some truly magnificent protective layer - however you'll require more assets to buy them.

At the point when you're prepared, search for the little unfinished plumbing space to one side of Sindri to enter the sanctuary, and prepare for an inviting party.

As you drop down into the long chamber, a Dark Elf Summoner will seem to do what he specializes in: Summon fortifications. He'll continue to do this as well, just as utilizing his weapon to send shockwaves and shots - so center shoot around him first prior to taking out the two Warriors that flank him.

At the point when they're dead, glance back at the divider you dropped down to thump a hanging pot down for some Hacksilver.

There's additionally a casket canvassed in roots here, and three throbbing centers on various strands along the lobby. Run past the most minimal one and pivot to throw your hatchet upwards at every one of them three, and you'll open the Coffin to get 1 Soft Svartalfheim Steel.

Further along the ring section you'll go over a large group of Exploding Nightmares. They're essentially heat-chasing rockets of toxic substance - get back and send off your tomahawks at them while evading the approaching Dark Elves. When your definite no more are coming, direct your concentration toward the mythical beings and rush and paralyze them to take them out.

You can't see the throbbing centers expected to open the final resting place as an afterthought, so bounce the hole into the following room and afterward head right until you can detect the line of three centers and hit them all to open the Coffin, and get back to get a Runic War Belt.

Back in the hazy room, go left and bounce up an edge and continue on until you come to a divider with handholds you can leap to.

This will lead you to the Ringed Temple Interior, where the Dark Elves take care of the light in hive of sorts. Move over to the foundation of the hive and draw in the Dark Elves here.

A Summoner is among them, so either dump on him rapidly or use Atreus to disturb him when he attempts to turn his staff and make more fortifications. You can likewise attempt to get behind them and knock them off edges for a fast kill.

At the point when the group lies dead, direct your concentration toward the root center and split it open prior to controlling up your hatchet deeply. It's not to the point of disposing of the hive, but rather it will project a sufficiently large shine to initiate an extension close by.

Cross the extension and head left, moving gradually for when a gathering of Explosive Nightmares show up. Wait and relax as they float to you, and use your hatchet tossing to explode them all from a protected distance prior to going up and crossing back to the middle.

More Nightmares will show up, as will a Dark Elf Summoner. Straightaway rush in and disturb his gathering and afterward continue to thump him into the divider to complete him rapidly before he moves the opportunity to move away. Kill different Nightmares and whatever other Elves who join the battle, then, at that point, search for another throbbing center to tear open.

Break Into the Hive
Coming up the incline subsequent to intersection the extension, you'll be at the entry to the hive - which is encircled by additional throbbing centers. Try not to be deterred, you just need to manage them in some ways.

Approach the one at the entryway, and go left to recognize a gathering of three you can hit in one go. Look above you to see the roots over that interface the following gathering of three and line them up too. At long last, line up the last three that closures with the entryway to totally dispose of the multitude of centers to acquire section to the Hive.

Inside the Hive, it's a genuinely close way. Veer through the opening and head up the incline to a divider you can move to the top. Continue to push ahead until you arrive at a low entry that will unintentionally take you directly to the focal point of the hive. Observe every one of the inhabitants as you quitely advance up the side.

Annihilate the Hive and Claim the Light
Profoundly. Hurl your hatchet and charge it as you did with the others.

At the point when the way disintegrates, hop down and prepare to battle through a swarm of Dark Elves. Fortunately these snorts will fall pretty speedy as Atreus will fix them before you. Utilize either Spartan Rage or your Runic Abilities to make a way before you, inclining toward charging assaults that present your.

Abilities like Whirling Storm additionally function admirably allowing you to avoid forward and assault to keep your foes under control. Close to the end when the way enlarges, go for moves like Invaldi's Anvil to beat back everybody around you to make the last push.

When you make a way deeply, obliterate it, and the sanctuary will become animated. Notwithstanding, before the undertaking is finished, Kratos should do something final to get the Bifrost imbued with the light.

As you enter the light, pursue the glimmering fire across a recognizable area until you arrive at the end. At the point when you return once more, pivot and search for a cavern to enter and climb a long divider until you arrive at the following way. Stroll forward, and the occasion will before long end.

At the point when you return, rejoin Atreus at the edge and utilize the Bifrost to implant his bow with Light Arrows - presently you will actually want to make light scaffolds any place you see the blue precious stones!

Physically focus on the blue gem from a remote place and have Atreus shoot it to make a scaffold across. On the opposite side, drop down to a lower level and glance around. There's a blue precious stone here yet it's been thrown away, and you can convey it to both of the containers here.

To get a bonus prior to leaving, note the casket over the center repository and spot the precious stone there, and you'll make a scaffold associating the upper walkway. Presently you can get to the final resting place and open it for a last Fragmented Heart of Alfheim Enchantment.

Return down to the lower level and put the precious stone on the repository close to the enormous roots impeding more gems, and it will make a scaffold back to the focuses lower level. Cross it, and manage a couple of Nightmares prior to heading left.

There's a chest here, and assuming you remain to one side of the first throbbing center you can detect another behind the roots to hit both, netting you a Hacksilver Chest.

Presently head under the roots to the opposite side of the stage to track down one more extension to make back to the external ring.

A couple of Dark Elves will attempt to stop you by shooting shots - stagger them with a hatchet throw and close the distance to knock them off edges.

Make one more extension under the roots and think back to adjust every one of the three throbbing centers, and you'll have opened up a way to make a scaffold to the exit. Fortunately, one more center on the middle island can be scattered to uncover a make to climb laugh out loud back to the top.

Back at the Light, one more team of Dark Elves will attempt to trap you. Recall that you can now redesign Atreus' Skills with the Light Arrows to increment stagger harm or debilitate adversaries to utilize his new capacity.

The way forward is by all accounts obstructed by a mass of light, however assuming that you look into you can detect a blue precious stone hanging like a pendulum. Look along the chain for a piece you can focus with your hatchet to break the chain and deactivate the divider.

Head up to the following room where the baffling blue entryway that impeded your advancement was before. It turns out there's a sand bowl on a more elevated level expected to initiate it however you'll have to make a way.

You can't hit the throbbing roots from this point, so return down to the Lore Marker and take the gem back up to this room. Place it on the main open space to have Atreus open a scaffold above it. Climb the stages to one side to get up to the higher vantage point and get over - offering you an ideal chance of the three throbbing root centers.

Drop down and place the blue gem in the recently opened spot. Try to bring up the image over the entryway, then, at that point, go around behind the gem to recognize a divider with an opening up the side you can support Atreus into. When he runs up and cuts the rune into the sand bowl, the exit plan will at long last be available to you.

Get back to the Boat

Assuming that you're in the disposition for sidequests, make certain to stop by Sindri's shop underneath to find out with regards to Fafnir's Hoard of fortune. In any case, head back along the scaffold towards the monster channel you opened - which means you'll have to take the long method for returning to your boat on the opposite side of the channel.

Utilize the lift on the option to return down to the jail region - and note that numerous cells are currently open...which may be fortunate or unfortunate. In any event, you can plunder the Hacksilver Chest.

As you head through the shut entryway into the primary body of the channel, you'll discover that somebody has set off its conclusion above you, projecting the channel into close dimness. The boat is currently at the opposite end, so proceed circumspectly. Two Poison Revenants will attempt to trap you, so ensure and use running assaults to follow up from Atreus shocking them and avoid around the toxin gaps they clear.

The precious stones down in this space are as yet inert, yet fortunately you have Atreus and his Light Arrows. There are two ways heading out to one or the other side of the channel room. Confronting the channel, the one on the right prompts a room with another precious stone repository and a locked entryway, so follow the left way all things considered.

In this little room you'll observe a lot of hindrances set off by a hanging gem. Hit it down with your hatchet and prepare to be trapped by Draugr from the various cells. They ought to be a weakling for you now, as long as you don't allow them to encompass you.

To evaluate a side riddle, get the blue gem and convey it as far as possible over to the contrary room with the repository. This will initiate the locked entryway, yet you'll require the right runes to open it, which are situated on four twirling instruments around you.

Immediately hit the sides with your hatchet until you observe the runes that resemble a "B", "E", a descending skewed "F" and a vertical skewed "F". Assuming you are too sluggish, the riddle will reset, however with training you'll have it opened instantly. Inside the treasury is a Coffin that holds Runic Scaled Spaulders and Soft Svartalfheim Steel.

Return the gem to the channel room and search for a lower stage with a repository for the gem. Use it to make an extension across back to where the long pathway to the sand bowl you previously brought down here is found.

You can really take a look at the cells close to the sand bowl for anything more you missed, and afterward prepare for a battle - as the head of the Dark Elf intrusion power won't allow you to leave easily.

Rout Svartalqfurr
This Dark Elf is extreme - however he essentially acts in much the same way to his companions. He jumps at the chance to dance around prior to running in with this spear to stick you or swing it in a wide circular segment, yet passes on a lot of opportunity to end up for you to either get ready to avoid, disturb or time a square without a second to spare to reeling him.

Inconvenience comes when he begins sending off shots. He'll much of the time run in reverse while abandoning shots for you to step on. In the event that you get hit, you'll be dazed, and assuming you thought this sucked previously, it's absolutely difficult to think that he is in the obscured field. You'll have to ease off and continue to avoid more shots until your vision returns - so watch for his assaults that send three shots into the ground across a wide region.

He'll likewise run back and plan to charge. At the point when he does this on the ground and you spot him coming, avoid aside or prepared a Runic Attack to disturb his charge. In the air, he's substantially more remarkable, and will ram into the ground sending a blinding shockwave that will compound the situation. In the event that you're now dazed, continue moving and evading until you have your sight back, and look to Atreus to sort out his overall position.

Use Atreus to keep him occupied while you run across and hit him with your Runic Attacks, and be prepared to counter his skirmish strikes or avoid in reverse assuming he establishes blinding explosives at your feet. You can't shock him, so center around bringing his wellbeing down and trying not to get dazed to keep in all out attack mode. Assuming you really do get dazed, avoid any unnecessary risk and continue to evade until you can see.

When he's out of wellbeing, play out a finisher on him to overcome this annoying fly for great. He'll drop an Etched Crest of Cunning Enchantment, just as a Runic Summon. This thing can be pervaded into Atreus' bow to bring monsters to help battle for you. It's on a cooldown very much like your Runic Attacks, and you can hold down the square button to actuate it in battle.

Get back to Midgard
Presently it's an ideal opportunity to at last abandon the sanctuary for great. Take the sand bowl lift up and out to return to your boat.

Assuming you're feeling like it and haven't investigated them previously, there's as yet the two far off shores to investigate for some genuinely speedy plunder:

Odin's Raven Location:

The Light Elf Shore is home to one of Odin's Ravens roosted on the platform of one of those Light Elf landmarks to one side as you enter. You can either throw your hatchet it from the ocean side, or from the gallery on the enormous tree.

Subsequent to getting out Draugr and Nightmare close to the ocean side, examine the goliath tree for a hanging box loaded with Hacksilver. There are three light precious stones installed in the ground you can hit to uncover a Realm Tear Encounter, which will set you in opposition to two more significant level double using Draugr. Dropping directly down the ocean side you'll track down a Hidden Chamber entryway to one side, and straight ahead prompts a passage. Here you can observe a chest obstructed by roots - cut the one over the hole and hop across, then, at that point, pivot to throw your hatchet through every one of the three.

The Light Elf Shore has some Tatzelwurms and gone Draugr sitting tight for you on the shore, just as a few roots on the left that block another entry. Kill the foes and search for an entryway at the far end and a switch that will raise the door - however just for a couple of seconds. On the opposite side will be two additional Tatzelwurms hanging tight for you.

Head back through the other entryway that is impeded by two roots. To raise it, hit the lower one so the door can raise, and before it pummels shut again hit the upper root and let the entryway crush the lower root.

Presently you can head onto a gallery sitting above the water where a Realm Tear is. This thing will bring two significant level Heavy Draugr to battle you, which can be somewhat hazardous considering the harm they bargain. Attempt to keep them isolated or dazed, and in the event that you can get the shock meter up on one of them, throw them into the water for a speedy kill. Overcoming the two of them will allow you Dust of Realms, which can be utilized to overhaul your Talismans.

Advance back to Tyr's Temple and sell your plunder at Sindri. Note that assuming you couldn't get a few things that were dropped in now difficult to reach region of the sanctuary, you can guarantee them in the Lost Items area from his menu.

Get once again to the sanctuary and utilize the Bifrost to advance back to Midgard, and to the Shore of Nine. Back in Midgard, you can converse with Brok about gathering his sibling, and he'll envy buff your weapon - just marginally. He likewise has new reinforcement to sell, and you can agree with him up on a particular position Favor: Second Hand Soul - an assignment to enter the Volunder Mines.

As you head across the scaffold to the Vanaheim Tower, you'll be assaulted by Speed Draugr. These folks aren't however a very remarkable sucker that ordinary Draugr, as they can run at you with rapid to hit before you can respond. Watch for their feet to touch off to flag a scramble and counter them when they come to assault.

Inside the pinnacle, you'll take note of the blue gems that embellish the inward dividers can now be shot - however be careful. This triggers a Realm Tear, a method for overcoming undeniable level adversaries to get Realm Dust to upgrade your Talismans. The adversaries you'd call would incorporate level 6 Revenants, who can probably kill you in a solitary hit at your present status, so you might need to hold off on those.

Legend Location:

Back inside the passage to the Foothills, the scaffold the Witch made is gone, compelling you to drop down. Presently you can track down a blue precious stone here - assuming you convey it to the container you can enact it to feature a Lore Marker: Beware of Seidr.

As you enter the Foothills, be careful an invasion of Rabid and Poison Wolves that will descend from the mountain to snare you. You can either head left and take Sindir's Skymover back up, or take the long far up - it's your decision. Head to the mountain way, and check whether the Light of Alfheim will serve you here.

Disperse the Black Breath
When incited, take out the Bifrost and use its light to beat back the obscurity. Gradually push ahead and the dull smoke will be pushed back as you advance up the way, and at the base, Kratos will at last scatter the Black Breath - and your way up the mountain will be clarified.

A NEW DESTINATION

Take Mimir's Head to the Witch

Since you have taken in the highest point of Midgard isn't your real objective, you'll have to track down a way to your actual objective, and the Witch of the Woods might have the option to help. Ideally.

As you head down the way, look off down the mountain and you can recognize the witch's woods - and surprisingly the circle of trees around your home!

Check to the left of the vista to observe a Hacksilver Chest, then, at that point, drop right down to a Mystic Gateway - the fastest (and just) method for getting down the mountain to Brok's Shop at Tyr's Temple.

Since you can utilize both Shock Arrows and Light Arrows, there's new regions to investigate and love to observe that wasn't accessible prior. To make up for lost time with all that you missed, you can backtrack up the Foothills and Mountain to get a few beforehand out of reach things.

What's more, the World Serpent has moved itself and has now roosted its head over the entry to Fafnir's Storeroom - would it be advisable for you decide to take part in that side mission. The waters of the Lake of Nine additionally hold many barrels and drifting bodies that can give you Hacksilver or Aegir's Gold assuming you draw near to them.

If not, steer your boat under the sculpture of Thor to get back to the Witch's Cave, since the water level has changed, the outing back will have been adjusted. At the point when you observe the new dock to the Witch's Cave, you'll observe a mass of World Tree Sap hanging tight for you. Hit the Shatter gem to cut a way ahead, and remember to enact the Mystic Gateway as well.

Take the lift up, and you'll wind up back in the chamber underneath the Witch's House. This moment is a decent opportunity to get a couple of things that were far off last time you were here:

Ensure you additionally invest in some opportunity to utilize the Shatter Crystal and make a scaffold to the Coffin to break the sap and gather Solid

Svartalfheim Steel and a Symbol of Perseverance You can likewise look to one side of the climbable divider prompting the Hidden Chamber to track down a dead body with Hacksilver.

The room with the Hidden Chamber additionally contains a chest Hacksilver Chest, a container of Hacksilver at the top, and a Coffin with Soft Svartalfheim Steel.

Treasure Map Location:

There's another thing to find in the Hidden Chamber entryway room - search for a little look close to the final resting place and have Atreus perused it to observe a Treasure Map! Assuming you can address the conundrum and find the lost fortune, you'll be compensated with a decent take of things - and the reference to a turtle should highlight an area close by.

Incredible Chest Location:

The blue roots nearby close to the Hidden Chamber seems to imply that you can do nothing more - except for you can. Admire the left of the thorn to spy flimsy wood that you can support Atreus up to.

He'll show up out on an edge, and you can move a bed of monster stones over to him to send him across to the opposite side where a sand bowl is. In the wake of reviewing it, gaze toward the roof to spy runes behind wooden sheets you can break with your hatchet.

As Atreus tackles the question, the stage he is on will lower, and you can hop across to observe a Legendary Chest in a niche that holds Murder of Crows - a Runic Summon for Atreus.

Get once again to the entry to the Witch's House just to observe the entryway hasn't brought - which means you really want down to observe a substitute way out. Fortunately, the monster beyond the red sap divider drives as far as possible back to the top.

Legend Location:

As you make the move up the well, have Atreus perused the runes to uncover a Rune Reading: Keep Out.

As you come out ashore, you'll be ignoring the monster turtle and the Witch's House just beneath you.

Legend Location:

Close to the neglect is a Lore Marker missing its text. Search for a blue precious stone reserved behind the well and bring it over to uncover the text of the marker: Prayer to Frigg.

Ancient rarity Location:

As you head down the way to the house, look to one side to observe the body of a dead trooper holding one of the Faces of Magic Artifacts, the Hole Mask.

Move to the front of the turtle, and you'll be trapped by a crowd of Draugr. The Shield Draugr specifically will run to and fro to hit you, while staying on high alert to repel and stun you assuming that you assault at some unacceptable time. Snare them into assaulting to counter them or break their protection with your safeguard and exploit their unbalance, and utilize Runic Attacks when more Draugr get involved.

Legend Locations:

Subsequent to killing the Draugr, make certain to search for two arrangements of Rune Reads: A Seidr Curse is beneath the bluff you descended from, while Down With Odin can be viewed as close to a chain up the side of a divider.

Treasure Map Solution:

Referring to The Turtle's Tribute treasure map you viewed as before, it specifies red leaves and green greenery, and the sketch shows the turtle alongside his front left foot. Head over to the front of his foot and search for a little way going by a few enormous stones, and watch out for a little overgrown stone close to it where the fortune is covered.

There's something else to investigate prior to heading inside the Witch's House.

Toward the left half of the turtle there's disintegrating rocks that have fallen over a Legendary Chest you can't get to - however there is a Sand Bowl with a conundrum to settle - and runes should be visible cut in the stones behind the scenes - yet you can't see them from here.

Ancient rarity Location:

A last ancient rarity can be observed climbing the chain close to the Rune Reads by the turtle. It prompts a short way with a dormant Nornir Chest, and in the event that you look to the side you can recognize another dead body holding the remainder of the Faces of Magic Artifact set!

Odin's Raven Location:

Admire the right from the dead body holding the last cover antique and you can recognize a ghastly green raven roosted on an enormous stone.

Amazing Chest Location:

Head to the furthest limit of the way past the raven to a disregard of the Witch's House that can allow you obviously to see every one of the runes upon the stones that settle the puzzle.

This will adjusted the disintegrating rocks to uncover the way to the Legendary Chest underneath them, and you'll acquire Storm of the Elks - a Runic Summon.

Since you've done everything around the Witch's House (her foundations actually block the section back to the remainder of the River Pass), it's an ideal opportunity to definitely head in... with your head. As the scene plays out you'll gain proficiency with a smidgen more with regards to your partners, and Mimir's head will return to life. After some laconic discourse, you'll be back in the cavern underneath the house.

Go to the Serpent's Horn
Head down the lift to the boat and take it as far as possible back to Tyr's Temple. Your true this time is the unusual horn that lies in the extension up a little lift. Head along the extension to the lift instrument to raise it up, and afterward have Mimir blow the horn to address the World Serpent.

After a short conversation that you don't become a piece of, the World Serpent will consent to help, and push the extension towards the Helheim Tower - and all the more significantly, a way to the two things you really want to venture out to Jotunheim: The Travel Rune, and an enchanted etch to cut said rune into the movement door back at the culmination of the mountain.

BEHIND THE LOCK

Return to the Boat

With the enchanted etch close by, all supernaturally fixed chamber entryways are presently unlockable - including the one to the side of the monster etch.

To do as such, you'll have to track down the highlight strike over the lock by coordinating the etch and afterward striking where the etch consumes most splendid.

In the room past, you can recognize a greater amount of the goliath's garments shaping a divider you can climb. There's likewise a Coffin encased in red sap - and assuming you look behind the frozen dress you can detect a Shatter Crystal you can wreck to free it netting you a Solid Svartalfheim Steel.

There's likewise a locked door utilizing Nornir Runes close by.

Look high over the entry way you rolled in from to detect the "C" looking rune.

Presently climb the gold studs of the attire to a high stage to the Dining Room, and think back across to see the "R" looking rune taking cover behind a monster clasp.

At long last, drop down the edge to one side and push as far as possible ahead and gaze upward over the clasp to see the "N" looking rune close to the highest point of the heap of ice.

This will open the entryway underneath to a dead Troll that holds a Glacial Catalyst - used to overhaul the Charm of Infinite Storm, a XP stone, and a Hacksilver Chest.

Get back to the Dining Hall and make certain to overhaul you Leviathan Ax to even out 5 - and buy any new abilities in the event that you really want to, or purchase/redesign any protective layer from your new riches, and afterward head out.

Drop down into the focal point of the Dining Hall and search for another mystically locked entryway to get through.

You'll be in a long lobby now, and off to one side is a final resting place secured by World Tree Sap. Up ahead is a blue precious stone container, and turning the corner right you'll observe the gem caught by more tree sap.

Take the main left to track down a text style of Shatter Crystal, and use it to free both the blue precious stone, and open the Coffin that contains Solid Svartalfheim Steel.

Presently take the blue precious stone to the platform and enact it to observe a Realm Tear, and communicate to get Dust of Realms (without battling any beasts). Head into the following region to track down a port with water in the center, and an exit under the goliath's thumb on the far side.

Go to the passed on first to observe a wheel component used to pull a lift across the top, and break the chain that holds it with your hatchet. Presently go right and have Atreus help up to the lift, and return to the wheel component to send him across the hole.

When it's at the far end, use your hatchet on the stuff over the lift to freeze it set up as Atreus wrecks a chain for you.

Move onto the lift and return your hatchet once again to ride it back to the opposite side. On the right, snatch a Hacksilver Chest, then, at that point, move left towards the exit.

Note that since you can open the Hidden Chambers of Odin, you can now investigate the one close here to observe a Jotnar Shrine for Thamur and one of Odin's Ravens - however more critically, the chamber prompts a kind of jail that houses a Valkyrie - an inconceivably strong miniboss that might be clearly past your ability now. Battle them just at your own danger, or return when you are all the more impressive.

Get back to Tyr's Temple

Heading back on the boat to Tyr's Temple, you can now investigate that supernaturally locked entryway at the foundation of the sanctuary that was as of late raised.

Assuming you'd prefer investigate first, you can return and look at every one of the Hidden Chambers of Odin you were unable to investigate previously - incorporating the ones found in The River Pass, the Foothills, Alfheim, and The Mountain - simply recollect that the Valkyries inside are not to be fooled with.

At the foundation of Tyr's Temple, go around the stage until you track down the supernaturally fixed way to open it utilizing the etch to hit the three ties and head inside.

As you enter Tyr's Bridge Interior, take a left to observe a Jotnar Shrine about Tyr that has been messed with, and a sand bowl question in the room. Atreus will tell Kratos the best way to do it this time - yet you'll be hindered before the example can start.

After the scene closes, Atreus needs some assistance, and just the Witch can assist with this. Ideally it's not past the point of no return.

THE SICKNESS

Ask the Witch for Help

With Atreus done for the count, you will not have the option to do anything but get him some assistance. Return back outside of Tyr's Temple and get on the boat advancing back to the Witch's Cave.

The skies have turned foreboding during your outing back to the cavern, and after taking the lift, you can hear that horn back at the sanctuary.

As you meet with the Witch, you'll discover that the main thing that can help your child is the core of the Bridge Keeper who directs the Bridge of the Damned - in Helheim, the domain of the dead. Your hatchet will be of no utilization against the dead - thus you will require another weapon: an instrument of Kratos' past.

Take the Boat to Return Home

There's very little you can do other than to follow the way given to you. Without Atreus your abilities are restricted as well - something to remember out and about ahead. The boat will guide itself as you advance back to the Wildwoods where your experience started.

When you show up at the boat moor that began your excursion, head up the natural way back to your hold home.

A gathering of Hel-Reavers have relocated to your patio while you've been gone - try not to take out your hatchet and get to punching. Without Atreus you can't stagger them with bolts, however Mimir will in any case make you aware of approaching strikes. Make utilize unarmed abilities like Guardian Sweep to wreck them and Guardian's Justice to develop a stagger meter to hold them back and stupefied - and take care not to take an excessive amount of ice harm.

Enter your home, and Kratos will recover the failed to remember relics of his past: The Blades of Chaos. Since you have them prepared, you'll have a fresh out of the plastic new Skill Tree to look at. You ought to have enough XP put away from your last excursion to purchase a couple of accessible abilities like Immolation and Rushing Chaos.

Likewise, your weapon tab will likewise have another space for your new weapons, however the frigid Runic Attacks you've tracked down so far can't be joined with the blazing edges.

Since you have new toys to play with, test them out on the swarms of Fel-Reavers that have amassed outside. The Blades of Chaos ought to be a gladly received and somewhat natural re-visitation of those mindful of Kratos' past undertakings. Assuming you're new to something like this - relax.

Generally, the Blades of Chaos fill comparative roles - rather than throwing your Leviathan Ax, you can heave the sharp edges like a lance and send them right back on your chain. You can likewise perform combos, and open running and avoiding assaults very much like the hatchet abilities.

Go to Helheim
Subsequent to killing all who remain before you, it's an ideal opportunity to make a beeline for Tyr's Temple. Fortunately, there's a Mystic Gateway in your patio, and since you can investigate nothing else, head on back through the World Tree.

As you return at Brok's Shop, you'll acquire the capacity to redesign the Blades of Chaos too - however you'll require an exceptional fixing to do as such, similar as the Leviathan Ax. Purchase or redesign as you want, then, at that point, head into the Realm Travel space to take the leap toward Helheim - the domain of the dead

Arrive at the Bridge Keeper
Helheim is a place where there is rankling cold and passing, so you'll have to utilize the red hot Blades of Chaos to their fullest degree to battle the chill. Truth be told, a few frigid Hel-Reavers and further developed Hel-Reaver Lords stand by along the Realm Travel Bridge to do fight - so utilize those edges.

As you approach the center of the extension you'll observe a greater amount of that agonizing Hel's Bramble that has dismissed you previously. Fortunately, with the flames of the Blades of Chaos these are presently not an issue, so get to pruning!

As you push ahead through a tight entry between the ice, new fast and dangerous undead will charge forward: the Hel-Brood, jumping huge spans or hopping high up to crush down on you. Fortunately, they don't have much in the method of safeguard, and you can evaluate your Spartan Charge to crush them to pieces.

Make certain to look appropriate for some Hel's Bramble that is hindering a Hacksilver Chest. Another Hacksilver Chest looks out for an edge above you to one side, yet you'll have to manage more undead and Hel-Shadow Archers first.

Slice through the Hel-Bramble and clear your path through the hordes of the dead to the goliath entryway into Helheim. It seems as though it's locked to the living, so you'll have to track down another way.

Look to one side of the way to see some Hel Bramble that can be pruned to uncover a way aside.

Subsequent to shimmying down a thin way, you'll end up in a little region with more Hel-Reavers, including protected adversaries. Like the Draugr, you'll either need to get through their watchman with your safeguard assault, or snare out their assault and counter. Be careful hitting when they have their gatekeeper up, as they'll circle back to an ice shockwave - however you can hinder its belongings on the off chance that you act rapidly.

Look aside of the space for Hel Bramble obstructing a Hacksilver Chest, and the opposite side to slice through more thistle to arrive at a climbable divider. Go moving around the points of support and down the opposite side into an enormous yard underneath.

Down here, rapidly turn around to take out the Hel-Reaver Archers, and afterward think back up between the support points to recognize a Hacksilver Chest caught by Hel Bramble.

Hit it with your Spear of Chaos on the two sides of the support point to free and wreck it. Additionally look against the back divider for more thistle up a precipice that is caught some Hacksilver you can get.

Moving further into the lower region, the ground will out of nowhere drop out as a Hel-Viking shows up with his goliath mace. Since you don't have Atreus to occupy him, take a stab at avoiding around behind his swings and hitting with weighty assaults on his unguarded side, and circling back to your Runic Attack for gigantic harm. You'll need to complete him rapidly before more Hel-Reavers appear at the contrary side of the pit, and afterward charge them utilizing your turning cutting edges to hit every one of them without a moment's delay.

In the wake of killing everybody in the pit, obliterate the thistle around you to track down multiple ways up. The bluff to the ice burrow is barely too far now, so take the move up beneath the tall scaffold all things being equal. Go to one side and search for more brier to obliterate, making a point of support tumble down and fill in as an edge to the next climbable divider from the pit.

Hop once again into the pit, and move up into an ice burrow that heads under more scaffolds to a tall climbable divider at the opposite end.

At the highest point of the edge you'll observe yourself to be simply beneath the primary way to Helheim, yet the street behind you prompts a Shatter Crystal in a mass of World Tree Sap that you can't detonate all alone. All things being equal, head forward and up one more edge that disregards the Bridge of the Damned, and an extraordinary monster bird that watches over the dead on their excursion.

Rout Mattugur Helson
For reasons unknown, the Bridge Keeper is one more variation of Troll that holds a supernatural weapon that recognizes the really dead. This weapon likewise makes him more fearsome than different Trolls you confronted, as he can utilize it to rapidly move around the field by disappearing and returning freely.

He'll likewise charge his weapon to leave behind drifting bombs that can incur a ton of harm assuming you're not focusing - yet since they move gradually, you'll have the option to move out of their reach when they explode or keep your safeguard up.

This savage will frequently substitute three weapon rushes while evaporating between assaults, finishing in a forward hammer you can avoid behind and afterward start your assault.

At the point when he magically transports off to security, watch for him to saturate a went shot impact that you can either avoid or take a stab at repelling to send back at his face.

In the wake of removing a piece of his wellbeing, he'll hammer you back towards the entryway and sit at the opposite end, beating his weapon into the ground that will convey little eruptions of dispersed shockwaves that can be bother. Run among them and sit tight for him to stop prior to racing into assault with a solid combo. Try not to stress over utilizing unarmed shocking assaults - he can't be paralyzed, so center around utilizing your Blades of Chaos.

After he withdraws once more, he'll probably begin gathering Hel-Broods to come and stop you, which is the reason you should adhere to utilizing the Blades of Chaos, as you can rush in and chain them all while as yet hitting the Troll toward the back. Do this a couple of times and he'll return to his ordinary assault design.

At low wellbeing, he'll likewise move to the opposite side of the field, and start swinging his weapon around behind him in anticipation of a major hammer assault - trusting that the somewhat late will magically transport and close the distance and throw his weapon down. In the event that you spot him moving his weapon around on schedule, you can be prepared to avoid around behind him and counter with a major assault, or utilize Spartan Rage to stun him.

He may likewise energize a few bombs before his turn, and his assault will send them surging in at his area.

Keep up the work avoiding behind his assaults or surging in when he stops his assaults and get out any augmentations he attempts to bring, and you'll at last have the option to stagger him long enough for the kill. Next comes the stomach assignment of getting his heart out, and your central goal here is finished. Make certain to plunder the Troll for a Chaos Flame - expected to overhaul your new weapons!

Get back to Midgard
Check out the field to reestablish your wellbeing and slice back some Hel

Bramble to get a Hacksilver Chest. The entryway back to the Realm Travel Gate has been fixed, and clearly you really want a the Winds of Hel to open it. Fortunate for you, such an ancient rarity is simply to one side of the entryway. Approach the green sphere and you'll get an update that allows you to store the Winds of Hel - yet just for a brief term.

Presently you can use wind traps found all over the domains to unlock specific regions, yet you'll should rush to track down them, as the breezes will return following 10 seconds.

Use it on the monster entryway to move the breezes, and afterward enter the enormous entryway.

On the opposite side, snatch the breezes again from the enormous entryway, and go to send them into the more modest entryway on the option to proceed onwards. A few Ice Nightmares will show up - yet you can rope them in with your Blades for a fast and simple kill. Note that the ways to the scaffolds above offer little without Atreus, so head to the following room and manage the Hel-Reavers that seem to stop you.

There's one more entryway on the contrary side of the entryway you rolled in from, however you can't snatch the Winds of Hel from this side of the entryway because of the ice. All things being equal, jump up onto the scaffold above and move towards the mass of Red Sap then, at that point, take a left onto a frigid edge and think down to recognize the breezes you can get from this point.

Run down to the lower stage and power the way to uncover a Coffin, which holds an Etched Crest of Providence.

To leave this region, fall to pieces the Hel Bramble impeding a little passage you can use to exit to the enormous entryway you found toward the finish of the sanctuary span.

It needs two Winds of Hel to charge the entryway - of which one is now embedded. Turn upward over the passage you emerged from to recognize the other one and set up it.

As you leave onto the scaffold and pass by all the dead - don't get diverted and miss the Hel-Traveler honing his tremendous cutting edge on the extension.

He might not have his safeguard, however he's as yet intense to harm, and can string together unblockable overhand assaults or stunning side breadths.

He may likewise bring his sword up in the air to charge - right away avoid in reverse as he released a huge shockwave around him, then, at that point, proceed with the attack.

Rout this extreme enemy, and you'll get his Deadly War Handles - new knob made to append to your Blades of Chaos. He'll likewise drop a greater amount of his defensive layer shards and war prizes used to make the Traveler Armor.

You might have likewise seen the little stone burial chamber close to the entryway ensured by a Winds of Hel repository. Since the entryway is open, it will not be requiring the two Winds of Hel, so assume one and position it in the stone way to uncover a Coffin with Solid Svartalfheim Steel.

With nothing left to do in Hell, it's an ideal opportunity to get back to the place where there is the residing. Enter the sanctuary to the Realm Transfer Room, and make certain to have Brok update your Blades of Chaos as you return to home base. Brok additionally has new knob for your sharp edge - so make certain to investigate tweak your new weapon, and buy new abilities.

Convey the Heart
Back in Midgard, Brok will illuminate you that he's overhauled the Mystic Gateways to allow you to head out to whatever other Mystic Gateway that you've opened - not simply back to Brok's Shop at Tyr's Temple. Test it out by taking the passage directly to the Witch's Cave.

Enter, and the core of the Bridge Keeper will recuperates the disorder that torments Atreus...for now.

MOTHER'S ASHES

Open a Passage to Jotunheim

After all that this experience has tossed at you, at last - the way to Jotunheim and your excursion's end looks for you. From Thamur's Corpse, utilize the Mystic Gateway to head out back to Brok's Shop at Tyr's Temple and go into the Realm Travel Room.

Set out to arrive at Jotunheim and think carefully to finish the movement into the domain of the monsters.

Abandoning Mimir, climb the means to enter the mountain range known as the Giant's Fingers - and make for the tallest pinnacle.

Inside the enormous chamber, have Atreus investigate the different sculptures and carvings to look into the monsters.

A divider on the right as you enter incorporates the Rune Reads: The Dream of Midgard.

Further up is another Lore mass of Rune Reads: The Guardian Returns.

As you head up to the leave, Atreus will uncover more wall paintings that portray an exceptionally fascinating disclosure.

From that point forward, it's an ideal opportunity to make a beeline for the pinnacle, and partake in the completion that follows.

Your principle excursion might be at an end, however the world actually allures with privileged insights and secrets. Make certain to head back the manner in which you came to Midgard and keep the experience going by looking at different missions to leave on:

8 Corrupted Valkyries are detained in both Midgard and different domains - these areas at the Hidden Chambers of Odin will presently be uncovered on your guide in the event that you haven't tracked down them.

Two explorable domains: Muspelheim and Niflheim, both proposition provoking journeys to overcome adversaries under testing situation, and can compensate you with astounding stuff.

Side Quests (Favors) from both the Dwarven Brothers and the Restless Spirits might in any case be dynamic and needing finishing.

Secret locales can be found in all edges of the Shores of Nine, and can conceal new collectibles like Legendary Chests, Nornir Chests, and Odin's Ravens.

GOD OF WAR ENDING EXPLAINED

Last Battle

During Kratos and Atreus' last fight with Baldur, the wild god becomes mortal subsequent to being pierced by the mistletoe that Sindri gave Atreus before on in the story. Turns out that the plant was the one thing that Freya couldn't guarantee couldn't hurt her child.

In Norse folklore, Freya (at times inseparable from Frigg. Lord of War's Freya appears to follow the hypothesis that Frigg and Freya are one in the equivalent.) requested everything in existance to vow a pledge to never hurt Baldur. She just didn't ask a mistletoe plant, considering it to be either excessively youthful, or irrelevant. It was Loki who looked for the mistletoe, shaped a bolt from its branch, and provided for Baldur's visually impaired sibling Hother to accidentally toss at Baldur with the remainder of the divine beings as they tried his resistance. This killed Baldur immediately, the main indication of Ragnorak.

This shortcoming permitted Kratos to snap Baldur's neck lastly put an end his frenzy. While Kratos and Atreus view this go about as essential, Freya watches her child kick the bucket with sickening dread, and pledges to get retribution in this inconceivable discourse which demonstrates that there is no more fearsome beast than like a mother disdained.

With Baldur far removed and Freya legitimately irritated, our legends are at long last allowed to utilize the Bifrost to head out to Jotunheim (with a touch of unpredictable assistance from Mimir).

The Mural Explained

As the pair advance up to the most elevated pinnacle, Kratos opens up the gauzes around his wrists, at long last reconciling with the apparitions of his past. He likewise at last permits Atreus to convey Faye's remains up the last stretch of the mountain, showing exactly how far these two characters have come.

The pair come to a sanctuary that the monsters developed in the wake of leaving Midgard. Unexpectedly the dividers give method for uncovering a mind boggling wall painting that prompts an alarming disclosure. A wall painting, that shows their past, present, and future, all working out without a moment's delay. From whenever Kratos and Atreus first met The World Serpent, to their battle with Baldur - - Atreus whole life is shown on the divider.

Faye was a Giant, implying that Atreus is part Greek God, and part Giant. Keep in mind, Giants are known so that their capacity might be able to see what's to come. As Kratos says, he wasn't the main parent leaving well enough alone.

After Atreus leaves the sanctuary, Kratos looks as a drape blows back, uncovering that the wall painting additionally shows what's to come.

Alright Kratos alone sees this last, covered up sheet, which is available to a touch of translation. Maybe Kratos is biting the dust, with his child nearby. In any case, what is emerging from Atreus' mouth? Does the kid cause Kratos' passing? Is the pattern of a child killing his dad genuinely not broken? Is it essentially Atreus hearing Kratos' last words? Also for what reason is Kratos so happy with this unfavorable picture? Tragically, we don't have deals with serious consequences regarding this.

Who is Faye and Atreus
So this is the place where things get interesting. We should get out ahead a couple of seconds to the uncover that the name Atreus was offered to the kid to pay tribute to a courageous and kind Spartan that Kratos knew back in Greece.

We discover Faye wished to name Atreus Loki, and that is the way she alluded to him to individual monsters, and in the wall painting. The kid's genuine name is Loki. Indeed, THAT Loki. Prankster, father of wolves (Fenrir), World Serpents, and Hel. What's more obviously, the impetus of Ragnarok - the demise of Baldur is the main domino that causes it in folklore.

We discover as the credits roll that Faye is otherwise called Laufey (Lau[faye], see?) Laufey is a jotunn (monster), mother of Loki, and spouse of individual jotunn Farbauti in Norse mythos. Laufey's moniker was Nal - perhaps importance needle - on the grounds that she was known to be little and thin when contrasted with other jotunn.

Who is Kratos in Norse Mythology

Similarly as Atreus' name was composed diversely in the runes on the painting, Kratos is as well'. The monsters' name for Kratos, in runes, is by all accounts Farbauti.

Farbauti in Norse Mythology is the spouse of Laufey, and is known as "Horrible Striker," connected with rapidly spreading fires. His legend isn't close to as broad as Loki's, however a few stories transfer both Farbauti and Laufey as dying right off the bat in Loki's life, and Loki getting taken on by Thor or Odin.

The True Ending

Since the credits are rolling, that doesn't mean the game is finished. Head back to your home after these underlying credits to trigger one more cut scene.

At the point when Kratos and Atreus head back to their home, the pair set down to rest after their long experience. Without precedent for the game, it slices to dark, uncovering a title card that peruses "A long time later... " Suddenly they're stirred by a savage tempest seething outside. After it removes the top of the lodge, Kratos goes outside to defy a hooded stranger encompassed by popping lightning.

The breeze catastrophes for uncover Thor's notorious sledge Mjollnir. Considering that you killed his two children, it's not hard to envision the reason why the God of Thunder has come thumping.

In the wake of Defeating All Valkyries

Be that as it may, stand by. There's as yet one final mystery in God of War, and that comes after you've crushed the 8 Valkyries just as what you accept that was the Valkyrie Queen.

GOD OF WAR NIFLHEIM - QUESTS, MAZE, AND ITEMS GUIDE

How the Maze Works

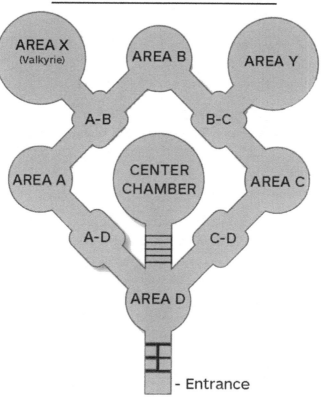

The labyrinth is procedurally produced which implies that the regions you visit reset each time you leave the labyrinth. Your objective in the labyrinth is to gather Mist Echoes from the chests all around the labyrinth.

The chests are in the open regions that are loaded up with undeniable level beasts - going from level 7 to 8, and all are exceptionally strong. You'll have to kill each of the beasts in a space to open the chests. Chests can likewise be found in secret areas between the devastating divider and sawblade traps. There are additionally Nornir chests in the labyrinth. There is one haphazardly produced Nornir Chest in the segments between the primary regions (A-B, B-C, A-D, C-D) where you need to hit the 3 ringers above you nearby. There can likewise be one more Nornir Chest in Area D which opens when you hit the rune switches above you in Areas A, B, and C to match the ones on the chest.

Assuming you kick the bucket in the labyrinth, you'll lose all of the Mist Echoes you've gathered since the last time you entered the labyrinth.

To forestall losing your Mist Echoes, leave the labyrinth from the entry close to Sindri's shop or move up the means to the Central Chamber of the labyrinth whenever you've opened it.

First Favor - Access the Central chamber
Addressing the Dwarves, you'll learn of a focal studio - situated in the focal point of the labyrinth simply past the principal genuine experience room. Sindri will make a Keystone to go into this room, yet solely after you get 500 Mist Echoes.

Fog Echoes can be acquired from every one of the chests you can find in the labyrinth, including a couple of found on the extension (One is situated behind a point of support to one side in the wake of leaving the shop, two are seen as close to the Lore Marker, and a chest and final resting place are situated close to the furthest limit of the scaffold). The most secure method for starting this errand is to run into the primary region, kill the foes and plunder all possible chests nearby, and run back to the entry assuming that you're coming up short on the meter.

On the off chance that you have sufficient meter left, you ought to likewise look at the two lobbies from the primary chamber - they are regularly loaded up with traps, yet assuming you are cautious you can go through them to observe chests and final resting places reserved as an afterthought, then, at that point, turn around prior to entering the following enormous chamber. Note that opening a chest will give a limited quantity of toxic substance meter back, permitting you to continue to move as long as you track down an adequate number of chests to make all the difference for you.

When you make the Keystone, return to the main chamber and rout the adversaries to utilize the Keystone on the focal special raised area, and enter the Central Chamber.

Second Favor - Search for Materials for Ivaldi's Protection
You'll observe a moderately protected region from the fog, which can fill in as another spot to rest between runs. It is additionally home to a few chests and Realm Tears that will become something of a primary objective here in Niflheim.

A portion of the chests and caskets are opened, and hold around 1,500 Mist Echoes - just as Ivaldi's Rusted Armor. There are additionally locked Legendary Chests and Realm Tears that must be opened when you have an adequate number of assets, and opening them will give you materials expected to specialty and overhaul Ivaldi's Armor - which can assist with easing back the impacts of the toxin mist, and will become urgent to getting by and crushing in this domain.

Get back to Sindri to find out with regards to what is expected to create the shield - and you'll find more fixings arbitrarily in the final resting places and chests while you investigate the labyrinth.

The excess secured chests in the Central Chamber can be opened with sufficient Mist Echoes to procure a few genuinely compensating things that reach from charms to weapon beats.

Chest Unlock Requirement	Reward
1,000 Mist Echoes	Perfect Artifact of the Blight - Enchantment
2,500 Mist Echoes	Eye of Niflheim - Enchantment
5,000 Mist Echoes	Chilling Mists of Niflheim - Enchantment (use to buy Frozen Flame at Dwarf Shop postgame)
7,500 Mist Echoes	Blightguard - Blades Pommel
7,500 Mist Echoes	Blightbringer - Axe Pommel

Third Favor - Seal the Three Realm Tears

There are additionally 3 Realm Tears - which contain very undeniable level adversaries who hold extraordinary awards for those adequately brave to confront them. Notwithstanding, they too need to ever be opened, and the cost is far more noteworthy.

Realm Tear Unlock Requirement	Enemies	Reward
10,000 Mist Echoes, 1 Anchor of Fog	Ogres	Mistborne - Axe Pommel
15,000 Mist Echoes, 1 Anchor of Fog	Wulvers, Soul Destroyer	Gift of Apollo - Blades Heavy Runic Attack
20,000 Mist Echoes, 1 Anchor of Fog	Revenants, Nightmares	Talisman of Cursed Power - Talisman

Notwithstanding an enormous measure of Mist Echoes, every Realm Tear needs an Anchor of Fog to open. You can observe these in unbelievable chests concealed in the two farthest offices of the labyrinth. Be careful about entering Chamber X on the grounds that there's a Valkyrie sitting tight for you.

Anchor of Fog Locations: The opportunity for a chest to contain an Anchor of Fog is arbitrary, so you should overcome whatever foes you find in those far chambers and check the substance of the chest just no doubt.

Step by step instructions to Grind in Niflheim

A huge piece of your time in Niflheim will crush - either to acquire Mist Echoes to open the money boxes in the focal chamber, or to crush for materials to art and overhaul the Ivaldi Armor Sets.

To do as such, you'll have to know what your capacities are: When you should keep investigating the mines, and when you should turn around and bank your Mist Echoes. Since foe levels range from 6-8, you'll as of now need to be solid going in.

NIFLHEIM MAP

Early runs should comprise of you remaining Area D (The beginning region) and after enduring the battle, search for any chests nearby, then, at that point, investigate regions A-D and C-D (the halls prompting Area An and Area C). Assuming you don't know you can endure different battles, these hallways are just loaded up with traps that you'll rapidly comprehend the rhythms, and you can dash through them to get extra chests.

When you're at a capable level (6-7), you ought to have the option to take on more battles unafraid of kicking the bucket. This ought to grow your investigation from Area D to Area An or Area C - yet you ought to forever be watching out for the pink meter. Chests can recharge this meter, yet it will be up to your judgment whether you can move forward to the following primary region or jump back to the entry - recollect battles can differ stunningly on schedule, so don't keep down on going all out with

Runic Attacks.

At the point when investigation becomes restricted exclusively by your capacity to stay in the toxic substance mist, you'll need to begin creating Ivaldi's Armor. Which shield you make first will to a great extent rely upon your playing style - however since you'll ultimately need to take out that Valkyrie, we reccomend either the Strength or Runic-centered covering to amplify your offense. With a decent arrangement of shield (and added charms or charms) you ought to have the option to endure significantly longer in the fogs, and do finish runs of the multitude of primary Areas A, B, C, and D.

Final plan investigation will take you to the external offices of Area X or Y. Region X contains the Valkyrie Hildr, and Area Y will contain genuinely amazing adversaries. Nonetheless, the greater they are, the better rewards you'll get. It's here that you get the opportunity to procure improved creating materials expected to update your covering, and things lik the Anchor of Fog - which can show up in an arbitrary chest around there, and is expected to open the last domain tears.

The Valkyrie - Hildr

Situated in one of the most distant offices of the labyrinth is the Valkyrie Hildr. She may not be the hardest Valkyrie you'll confront, yet the way that the toxin fogs are as yet present will make it an incredibly difficult match, as you'll have to kill her before the fogs kill you.

Do a couple of runs in Niflheim so you can open the chests in the storeroom and prepare charms that will keep you alive longer in the fog.

The super new assault you want to look out for is her ice assault, which ought to be obstructed, and afterward avoided toward the end when she fires that monster icicle. In the event that she monitors herself with her wings, use your Block Break expertise to drop her defenses.

Recollect that regardless of whether you use up all available time you'll in any case live for a couple of seconds as your life begins depleting - and assuming you can kill Hildr in this occurrence, your meter will be recharged from the kill after the cutscene.

GOD OF WAR DRAGONS - WHERE TO FIND DRAGON TEARS

Investigate God of sufficiently war and you'll track down Dragons. There is three all out to find, and each offers a Dragon Tear inasmuch as you set them free. The following are the God of War Dragon areas and how to observe each Dragon Tear (counting where to observe the last Dragon Tear) in God of War for creating and updates.

Spoilers for winged serpent areas follow!

To free winged serpents you'll have to find and annihilate three holy places in a space to break the seal on the anchor keeping the mythical beast binded. The mythical serpents are recorded in the request you're ready to get to them, and connections to their total walkthrough have been given. Walkthroughs are not presented on this page on limit spoilers.

Veithurgard Dragon

This first mythical beast can be gotten to when Kratos comes to the Lake of Nine. However, to get to Veithurgard, Kratos needs to open a monstrous brilliant entryway. Do as such by going to Stone Falls and twist the wheel close to the orange soul that gives you the Hammer Fall favor.

Bounce back in the boat and column toward the remnants of Veithurgard. Dock on the shore and take out the foes that look out for the rough ocean side. There's a Lava Ancient here as well, so be cautious while connecting with this battle. After you clear the region, climb the precipice to track down a shop and a Lore Marker. Forge ahead, battle a few wolves, then, at that point, bounce in another boat. In the lake you'll see Thor's sculpture on the left and a dock for certain remains around on the right.

Column up and dock on the right. Battle through the couple of adversaries here. Finish the way the vestiges to track down the mythical beast, yet don't stroll up the means excessively fast! This monster is irate. It'll kill a light emission and lightning the line, so approach it with alert and stow away in the side entries to keep away from its assaults.

Track down the three places of worship nearby and obliterate them to free the winged serpent Otr. Utilize this manual for think that they are all. After you free the winged serpent, it'll drop a Dragon Tear.

The Lake of Nine Dragon

Line north toward the two monster sculptures of men paddling boats. To one side is an edge covered by plants and tree sap. Dock, then, at that point, have Atreus use shock bolts to obliterate the briers. Climb the divider and advance toward the enormous wooden way to track down the following mythical beast.

Likewise with the other mythical serpent, break the three places of worship to eliminate the seal on the fundamental anchor that keeps the mythical serpent binded. Compelte this to get the Dragon Tear and an uncommon improvement called "Splendid Scale of the Chained."

Konunsgard Dragon

This winged serpent is just open after you complete a set number of side journeys.

For a total walkthrough with nitty gritty data on the most proficient method to free this mythical beast, visit The Fire of Reginn walkthrough.

The last mythical serpent needs your assistance is in Konunsgard. You can arrive at this area subsequent to opening the Hail to the King favor. Do as such by completing all of Brok and Sindri's blessings. Assuming you haven't done any at this point, it may invest in some opportunity to get to this blessing.

When you have the Hail to the King favor, you can observe Konunsgard by entering through King's Hollow which is to one side of the Light Elf Outpost through a cavern. You can likewise follow the blessing now. When you come to the yard of the primary structure in Konunsgard Atreus will recognize the winged serpent farther back on the property. There are huge loads of adversaries around here, so be ready for a very long time en route to the winged serpent.

After you arrive at the mythical beast you can begin bringing down the three fixing holy places after you pass it. Get the areas of the multitude of hallowed places on The Fire of Reginn walkthrough page. Likewise with the other two mythical serpents, Kratos gets a Dragon Tear for liberating the monster alongside different merchandise.

Last Dragon Tear Location

This Dragon Tear must be found assuming you've made it a respectable way through God of War's primary storyline. Snap or tap the spoiler button beneath to uncover precisely when you can track down it.

LEGENDARY CHESTS

The River Pass Legendary Chests

Stream Pass Chest 1

Directly down the way from where you battle a Reaver prior to intersection the extension that breakdowns, Atreus will call attention to a chest on the right. It contains a Runic Gem: Hel's Touch.

Stream Pass Chest 2

In the wake of entering the Witch's Cave interestingly, head down the scaffold and go left across stages to a boat. As you jump across the stone stages, make a point to plunder the Legendary Chest toward the end for a Talisman of Concentrated Vitality.

Waterway Pass Chest 3

Subsequent to getting both Light and Shock Arrows, return to the Witch's Cave. Head to the base floor and make ways utilizing Light Arrows to a mass of sap you can break with adjacent Shatter Crystal.

Head into the region to one side of the Hidden Chamber of Odin. The blue roots seems to imply that you can do nothing more - except for you can. Admire the left of the brier to spy brittle wood that you can support Atreus up to.

He'll show up out on an edge, and you can move a bed of goliath stones over to him to send him across to the opposite side where a sand bowl is.

In the wake of reviewing it, gaze toward the roof to spy runes behind wooden sheets you can break with your hatchet. As Atreus addresses the enigma, the stage he is on will lower, and you can hop across to observe a Legendary Chest in a recess that holds Murder of Crows - a Runic Summon for Atreus.

Stream Pass Chest 4

In the wake of getting the past chest, obliterate the Red Sap Wall and move up the well to the backwoods around the Witch's House. There's a Legendary Chest on the opposite side of the huge turtle, canvassed in rubble, just as a sand bowl.

Search for a chain to move up to an edge and head to the furthest limit of the way past the raven to a disregard of the Witch's House that can allow you evidently to see every one of the runes upon the stones that address the enigma.

This will adjusted the disintegrating rocks to uncover the way to the Legendary Chest underneath them, and you'll acquire Storm of the Elks - a Runic Summon.

Stream Pass Chest 5

After you get the thing expected to associate with the Winds of Hel, head down to the Witch's Cave, and head to one side of the well to where the Cipher Chest was to track down Hel's Wind, and get it. Take it to a container to one side of the extension to the Witch's House, then, at that point, down underneath to the solitary stage in the lower cave region. Cross to the opposite side of the cavern to put the breeze on an upper stage over some Hel Bramble. Then, at that point, annihilate the brier and move the monster bed of stones to the center so you can get the Winds of Hel and hop across to the opposite side and spot it in a stone vault, which will uncover a Legendary Chest holding the Rampage of the Furies - another Light Runic Attack.

Shores of Nine Legendary Chest
As you descend down to the outer ring of Tyr's Temple, sprint around to the Northwest side facing Asgard Tower to find a Legendary Chest surrounded by Hel Bramble. Break it apart to open the chest and receive Weightless War Handles - Rare Blades Pommels for your Blades of Chaos.

Iron Cove Legendary Chest
There is one Legendary Chest to find at the Iron Cove, accessible once the waters have subsided from the Lake of Nine two times.

Climb the way dependent upon the top stage to observe a fixed Rune Door covered with Scorn Poles. Every one of the Scorn Poles conceals red urns close to them you can explode, and afterward take out the Poison Wolves that watch the entryway.

To open the Rune Door, you'll have to hit the different rune systems to match the fixed entryway similar as a Nornir Chest. To observe the principal seal, look left from the way back to the old upper harbor towards the front of the destroyed boat, and you can recognize a system you can turn to a rune that resembles a "B".

Get back to the destroyed boat and search for a red urn under the boat close to a Scorn Pole you can detonate. Move up to the highest point of the boat, and peer down to one side to detect one more rune component down where the East harbor was and match the "p" looking rune.

At long last, hop across to the opposite side of the destroyed boat, and look left over the side of the boat to recognize red urns behind the last covered rune component. It just has one oar, so head down to the passed on side of the rune and match it to the "E" looking rune to open the fixed Rune Door.

The Legendary Chest for the Mists of Helheim - a Heavy Runic Attack for your hatchet, just as Pristine Ore of the Realm, an asset just saw as here.

Isle of Death Legendary Chests
There are two incredible chests situated on the Isle of Death. One requires a later game overhaul, while the other requires the waters of the Lake of Nine to have gone down two times.

Isle of Death Chest 1

When the waters have gone down two times, advance back up to the highest point of the island where the first shore was.

When back at the highest point of the Isle of Death, stroll under the boat destruction and slide down the rope to arrive at the principal Legendary Chest. Inside is an uncommon hatchet pulverize called Ymir's Breath.

Isle of Death Chest 2
The last Legendary Chest on the Isle of Death was presumably one of the

main collectibles you spotted after visiting. The chest is shrouded in thorn close to the brazier from the blessing Unfinished Business. Basically utilize the Blades of Chaos to consume the thistle and acquire the Explosive Grips of Fire - a Legendary Blades Pommel.

Stone Falls Legendary Chests

There are 2 Legendary Chests situated at Stone Falls, and one will expect you to re-investigate the region once the waters of the Lake of Nine have gone down two times.

Stone Falls Chest 1

When you show up at the dock whenever the waters first go down in the Lake of Nine, move straight forward tp a chain that lifts the entryway. However, while lifting up the door, one behind the scenes closes.

There is a way around that you can open simply ahead. Kill the Revenant and Wurms on the opposite side and afterward look toward the raised scaffold. Toss your hatchet at the anchor highlight bring down the extension. Return the chain and lower the nearest entryway. Presently utilize the scaffold to go around.

Get back to the area you battled the Revenant to track down the lifted entryway. Open the Legendary Chest inside to capture a Golden Talisman of Protection.

Stone Falls Chest 2

At the point when the waters of the Lake of Nine have gone down two times, return to the Stone Falls to observe monster wheels canvassed in red sap.

Utilizing the water wheel inland, you can shoot the sap to break the covering on the chest. Inside is an Ax Pommel called the "Dangerous Grip of Fury."

Veithurgard Legendary Chest

There is 1 Legendary Chest situated in Veithurgard, a region you can get to by utilizing the wheel instrument at the Stone Falls.

Clear your path through the Veithurgard Keep until you should delivery and rout the Fire Troll. He jumps and steps the ground to shoot out magma waves. Utilize hatchet tosses when the magma is erupting out of the savage's feet. Go in to bargain weighty harm when the fire has cleared. Utilize runic assaults or Spartan Rage to interfere with any steps that surprise you.

Overcoming the Troll will drop a key that is for the enormous swinging doors toward the rear of the chamber. These lead to a Legendary Chest with the Light Runic Attack "Leviathan's Wake" inside.

Lower regions Legendary Chests
There are 2 Legendary Chests situated in the Foothills.

Lower regions Chest 1

When you show up in the cold remains before the mountain where you battle an Ogre, seek the left side for a heap of rubble close to a red urn you can explode to clear the garbage.

To one side of the casket are two Scorn Poles and another urn you can impact across the hole - yet both of shafts are similarly obstructing the Legendary Chest here. Freeze the one nearest to you to detect a urn behind the other, and explode it to dispose of one of the posts. This permits you to freeze the excess one and open the chest to get the Charge of the White Bear, a Light Runic Attack.

Lower regions Chest 2

This Legendary Chest must be acquired once you have the apparatuses to cooperate with the Winds of Hel and get out the Hel Bramble.

Head up the way from Sindri's Shop up the divider along the way fixed with Scorn Poles. To one side of the way driving up is a stone burial place that has been fixed. Assuming that you admire the left you can detect some of Hel Bramble impeding a container, yet it has no wind.

Head down to the way to the region for certain final resting places to observe the Winds of Hel caught behind some Hel Bramble and remove it, then, at that point, convey it to the stone burial chamber to open it, allowing you to open a Legendary Chest that contains the Blast of Hephaestus - a Light Runic Attack.

Alfheim Legendary Chests
There are 5 Legendary Chests situated in the domain of Alfheim.

Alfheim Chest 1

When you initially enter the Ringed Temple Trench, check the phone rooms on one or the other side of the lift.

One of the rooms has a wrecked system, yet the other can be utilized to open the enclosures. Really take a look at the cells here to track down Hacksilver on a cadaver in one room, and the other room has an obstructed way to a chest you can see from this point.

Toss your hatchet at the root over the chest, then, at that point, leave back to the middle room and investigate the cell from the hindered entryway.

Bring your hatchet back and it will hit the two roots returning, opening the entryway and permitting you to plunder the Legendary Chest for Thiazi's Talon, a Heavy Runic Attack.

Alfheim Chest 2

This Legendary Chest can be found on the stage underneath the really light scaffold prompting the sanctuary. It very well may be found on the passed on side of this stage after the fight to get out the roots hindering the light gem above, and you'll observe it holds Njord's Tempest, a Light Runic Attack.

Alfheim Chest 3

Whenever you have reestablished the Light of Alfheim, move around the sanctuary center to dispose of the roots and reestablish the extension back to the principle entrance. Deeply, have Atreus focus on the recently uncovered precious stone on the top ring to make another extension to the entryway.

Here a couple of more Dark Elves will attempt to impede you, and they watch a close by Legendary Chest that holds Strike of the Utgard, a Light Runic Attack.

Alfheim Chest 4

Out on the lake that encompasses the Ringed Temple, take the boat up toward the Northwest ocean side to the Light Elf Shore. Search for a way to the right that leads into a long passage past certain roots.

At the opposite finish of the passage from the gathering of roots, head out onto the stage sitting above the ocean side to observe a Legendary Chest holding Frost Giant's Frenzy - a Heavy Runic Attack.

Alfheim Chest 5

Take the boat over toward the Southeast side of the lake to the Light Elf Sanctuary. An entryway on the left of the ocean side is encircled by roots, so get to higher ground by passing through the door and afterward close to an overhang sitting above the lake back to an extension over the ocean side.

Cross the scaffold and peer down to detect a point to hit every one of the roots on the double.

With the roots gone, there's another passage to the side you can take into a little room with a Legendary Chest covered by three throbbing centers close by - two of which are on independent hanging bars.

Utilize the close by wheel instrument to turn the bars as far as possible, and watch as they pivot back leisurely to adjust while confronting the main fixed center at the top.

Hit them as they line up with a hatchet toss. This will open the chest to uncover the Amulet of Kvasir - an uncommon Talisman that eases back time upon wonderful evades.

Fafnir's Storeroom Legendary Chest
There is 1 Legendary Chest to find at Fafnir's Storeroom during the Fafnir's Hoard journey.

Fafnir's Storeroom Legendary Chest

114

There is 1 Legendary Chest to find at Fafnir's Storeroom during the Fafnir's Hoard mission.

Volunder Mines Legendary Chest
There is 1 Legendary Chest to find in the Volunder Mines, during the Second Hand Soul journey.

When you enter the mines, you'll ultimately confront the "chief" of the region - a Soul Reaver. Annihilate it by assaulting its uncovered chest and tossing the hazardous rocks back at it until it is staggered.

When the Soul Reaver kicks the bucket, look along the edge of the field for the Legendary Chest that contains the Light Runic Attack "Fierceness of the Ice Troll".

The Mountain Legendary Chests
The Mountain Chest 1

When you observe the mine truck expected to make a lift up the mountain in the focal lift room, push the minecart until you can make a stage to the upper region where the stone has stalled out. As you pass along the upper stage, look along the left side for a Legendary Chest that contains Falcon's Dive - a Runic Summon for Atreus.

The Mountain Chest 2

Subsequent to overcoming the Dragon on the mountain and acquiring Shock Arrows, enter the new entryway past Sindri's Shop.

As you enter this new cavern, turn right and you'll observe World Tree Sap encasing a Legendary Chest in a little rooms. Have Atreus shoot it with his shock bolts to open the chest, and gain Tyr's Revenge - a Light Runic Attack

The Mountain Chest 3

Upon your re-visitation of The Mountain, head back to the focal lift room and clear the Hel Bramble to utilize the auxiliary lift to another area. Here, you can scale a stage to one side to observe an entryway where an Ogre will blast out of.

In the room where the Ogre burst out of is a stone burial place fixed by the Winds of Hel. To track down these breezes, drop down to the level beneath and fall to pieces some Hel Bramble on a space to one side to observe a container you can convey.

Place it close to the foundation of the stage paving the way to the upper level, then, at that point, return to get through a wooden divider entryway close to the Hel Bramble to track down a chest of Hacksilver and the Winds of Hel.

Take the breeze to the repository you put, then, at that point, move up and snatch them from up top prior to running to the burial chamber to uncover a Legendary Chest that holds Hyperion Slam - a Heavy Runic Attack for the Blades of Chaos.

Thamur's Corpse Legendary Chest
While there are no recorded Legendary Chest in the Region Summary, there is 1 that is unlisted - and can't be gotten back to subsequent to getting through the ice.

In the wake of meeting Sindri at his first shop, head along the stages to a structure where you battle your first Traveler.

Subsequent to overcoming him, haul the enormous stone square out of the entryway and adjust it close to the hanging Giant's Pendant. Look at the edges for boards to toss your hatchet at to shift the pendant aside, then, at that point, leap to it in the wake of climbing the square.

From the pendant, move over it and hop down to an upper overhang to observe a Legendary Chest that holds Blessing of the Frost - a Heavy Runic Attack.

Light Elf Outpost Legendary Chest
There is 1 Legendary Chest in the Light Elf Outpost, a region that shows up after the waters of the Lake of Nine have brought down two times.

Utilize the light precious stones on the island to make ways that breeze around the island to the extremely top. At the highest point of the Light Elf Outpost, you'll observe the Legendary Chest that holds the Runic Summon: Bitter Squirrel, which gathers a phantom squirrel, Ratatoskr, to uncover consumables.

The chest will likewise deliver a Pristine Scales of the Realm, a Legendary material used to update strong protection, just saw as here.

Buri's Storeroom Legendary Chests
There are 2 Legendary Chests to find at Buri's Storeroom, an island that just shows up once the waters of the Lake of Nine have gone down two times.

Buri's Storeroom Chest 1

When coming to shore on Buri's Storeroom, you ought to have seen a huge Nornir entryway. You really want to ring three chimes to open the entryway. Two of the ringers are to the left and right of the entryway, separately. The third is taken cover behind a door to one side.

The best way to bring down the entryway is on its posterior, however that leaves you caught with no chance back to the entryway. Circumvent the rear to observe a piece of red sap that you can utilize shock bolts on.

Get back to the front and climb the steps to track down a recently liberated wheel. Turn it to pivot the waterwheel ahead and track down a tolerable hole. Presently return to your boat and line to the recently open ocean side.

Bring down the entryway and afterward line back to the front of the entryway. Each of the three chimes are out in the open at this point. Just ring every one of the three rapidly to open the entryway and uncover the Legendary Chest inside with the Heavy Runic Attack Glaive Storm inside.

Buri's Storeroom Chest 2

The last Legendary Chest is encased in brier that must be ignited with the Blades of Chaos. At the point when you return to Buri's Storeroom with the Blades, there will be level 7 and 8 Draugrs alongside a level 7 Traveler. You should kill them all to make the region sufficiently safe to snatch the chest. Inside is the Rage of the Titans light runic assault.

Helheim Legendary Chests
There are 3 Legendary Chest situated in Helheim - just as 1 extra Legendary Chest situated past the Bridge of the Damned.

Helheim Chest 1

From Tyr's Temple, approach the center of the extension prompting Helheim and you'll observe a mass of Hel's Bramble you can clean up. Look to one side of the Hel's Bramble to observe a Legendary Chest that contains Spartan Charge: your first Light Runic Attack for the Blades of Chaos!

Helheim Chest 2

After you have acquired the capacity to tackle the Winds of Hel, head back to the scaffold driving back to Tyr's Temple.

There's a little hand-off game you can play with one more Winds of Hel repository up on the right half of the scaffold. In the first place, get out the remainder of the Hel-Reavers along the length of the scaffold, then, at that point, return to put the Winds of Hel in the primary piece on the right.

Presently get it and raced to the chunk up on the left where you can stash it to renew your time. Snatch it again and run forward until you see a sculpture with a safeguard and a container in the center to put it in.

Snatch it again and get around the obstacle to the following sculpture on the right, and look on its back to put the Winds. Snatch it again and run over to the center of the extension where the enormous horn is, and turn upward along the inward ring to find one more spot to put the Wind.

Presently, yank the breezes back and run up along the passed on side of the scaffold to an impasse - where you can recognize a section to put the breeze again.

Go around to the opposite side of the piece and get it, and promptly run across the scaffold to the steps and search for a section above on the right before you go down.

At long last, head down to a lower gallery, turn left and toss it at the earliest opportunity as quickly as possible to open the stone seal to track down a Legendary Chest, and guarantee your award of Cyclone of Chaos, a Light Runic Attack for the Blades of Chaos.

Helheim Chest 3

You can track down this chest after getting back to Helheim with Atreus after he's better. Enter the principle way to the Bridge of the Damned and move up the primary upper stage with a small extension going right to a red mass of Sap.

Detonate it with shock bolts and search for a chain on the opposite side to drop down. Here you'll observe one more little mass of red sap can be detonated to arrive at a Legendary Chest that holds The Charm of Infinite Storms - an Epic Talisman.

Helheim Chest 4

However additionally not set apart in the locale rundown, you can observe a Legendary Chest during the Escape From Helheim mission when you are across the Bridge of the Damned. Whenever you have taken off on the boat, it will stall out on a stage and you should figure out how to free it. As you enter the actual pinnacle to observe a turning instrument you can toss your hatchet at to raise a stage.

Ensure your off the stage when you hit it, then, at that point, duck under to the overhang on the contrary side of the pinnacle to track down a Legendary Chest that holds Icarus Storm, a Light Runic Attack for your Blades of Chaos.

Tyr's Temple Legendary Chests
There are 2 Legendary Chests situated in Tyr's Temple.

Tyr's Temple Chest 1

In the wake of getting the Black Rune, two Grendels will assault you.

Since you've gotten out the Grendels, think back to the chamber that caught you to observe the stage has ascended to uncover a Legendary Chest in a nook, and open it to get Weightless Grips of Protection.

Tyr's Temple Chest 2

When you can enter Tyr's Hidden Chamber (not to be mistaken for Tyr's Vault), head down the lift to where the two chains should be broken.

Follow the passed on way through the corridor of turning edges to the room past, and search for a stone burial chamber on the left holds one of two Winds of Hel - while the lobby past it has a fixed saw sharp edge with a container for the Winds of Hel, and one more to the right.

Take out the Winds of Hel when the saw sharp edge is withdrawn to one corner to keep it that way, and return it to the stone burial place in the past chamber.

Presently cross past the sharp edge to see as one more with Winds in it, and return that to the stone piece also to open up a Legendary Chest that holds Hyperion Grapple - a Heavy Runic Attack for the Blades of Chaos.

Konunsgard Legendary Chest
There is 1 Legendary Chest in Konunsgard, a region that must be gotten to in the wake of finishing every one of the side missions for the dwarves until the two of them give you the Favor - Hail to the King.

Advance toward the fortress that is the object of the mission, and head to the royal chamber.

Toward the finish of the room is the bantam ruler's high position. Push it to the side to track down the ruler himself alongside the things you came looking for. Make a point to snatch the legend look by the lord's cadaver prior to proceeding back outside through the mysterious passage the ruler had made.

Back outside, follow the way underneath a cascade to observe a Legendary Chest simply holding up out in the open. Inside is the Prometheus Flame, a weighty runic assault for the Blades of Chaos.

ABOUT THE AUTHOR

I When I finding new tricks, tips, and strategies to beat each other, they came up with a brilliant idea. Let's take these hours of gaming expertise, and share these skills with like mind people. At that moment, the God of War Complete Guide & Walkthrough were born. With more exciting gaming books being developed in the Lab as we speak. I am creating a buzz in the gaming guide publishing world, with a ground swell of followers, anxiously awaiting my new releases.

Made in the USA
Monee, IL
19 May 2022